A GUIDE TO
WATER GARDENING

A Guide To
Water Gardening

PHILIP SWINDELLS

CHARLES SCRIBNER'S SONS

New York

Contents

List of Illustrations

PHOTOGRAPHS

LINE DRAWINGS

ACKNOWLEDGEMENTS

Laurence E. Perkins: photographs 1, 2, 10, 23-30
Harold Langford: 3, 4, 6, 7, 8, 9, 11, 12, 13, 15, 16, 17, 18, 19, 20, 22
J. E. Downward: 5, 14, 21

Introduction

'Advice to those about to build a water garden—DON'T.' Thus wrote one of the greatest horticulturists of all time, Reginald Farrer, in his undisputed classic *Alpine and Bog Plants* (1908). The celebrated landscape gardener, William Robinson, was of the same opinion, writing in his *English Flower Garden* (1895): 'Unclean and ugly pools deface our gardens; some have a mania for artificial water, the effect of water pleasing them so well that they bring it near their houses where they cannot have its good effects. But they have instead the filth that gathers in stagnant water and its evil smell on many a lawn.'

Happily today we understand a little more about the successful construction and management of water gardens than Farrer, Robinson and their contemporaries. Consequently, the garden pool is becoming a prominent feature of many gardens, providing a cool retreat where on a warm summer evening one can escape the pressures of modern living and relax with just the gentle murmur of moving water for company. Furthermore, its enjoyment is not restricted to the fortunate few with unlimited space. Even those of us who through necessity are often restricted to suburban patches in sprawling conurbations can accommodate a water garden of surprising grandeur. A garden pool, no matter what size, is never insignificant if well arranged and in conformity with its surroundings. A single diamond is not comparable with the regalia of a maharajah, but it is a diamond just the same.

Glossary

AMPLEXUS Amphibious mating act appertaining particularly to the toad and frog.

ANAL Situated near the anus.

AXIL Angle between stem and leaf base.

BARBEL Small fleshy appendage.

BRACT A leaf in the axil of which a flower arises.

CARAPACE The shell that covers the back of a tortoise or terrapin.

CAUDAL Near the tail.

COMPOSITE Of the natural order *Compositae* (Daisies etc.).

CORDATE Heart-shaped.

CRUSTACEAN One of the natural order *Crustacea* (crabs, prawns etc.)

CULTIVAR A named cultivated variety of plant.

CYPRINID A member of the *Cyprinidae* or carp family.

DENTATE Toothed.

DORSAL Near or belonging to the back.

EXCRESCENCE An abnormal protuberance.

FLACCID Soft or flabby.

GENES The hereditary factor which is transmitted by each parent to offspring and which determines hereditary characteristics.

GLAUCOUS Sea-green, covered with a fine bloom.

GONOPODIUM Male reproductive organ in certain tropical species of fish.

HERMAPHRODITE Bisexual.

HIRSUTE Hairy.

INFLORESCENCE The arrangement of a group of flowers.

LAMINA The blade of a leaf.

LANCEOLATE Lance-shaped.

MILT Sperm bearing fluid of certain fish.

MONOTYPIC One only, particularly referring to a genus containing only one species.

MUTANT A plant or animal which differs from its parents as a result of a genetical change, usually without any visible external influence.

NAIAD A nymph.

NODE Leaf joint.

OCTAPLOID Having four times the basic chromosome number.

ORBICULAR Spherical.

OVA The female germ cells.

OVARIES Pertaining to the ovary which contains the ova.

OVATE Egg-shaped.

OVIPOSITOR Egg laying organ.

OVOID Egg-shaped.

PECTORAL On or near the chest.

PETALOIDES Brightly coloured and resembling petals.

PISTIL Female reproductive organ in a flowering plant.

PLASTRON Breast-plate.

PROCUMBENT Lying loosely along the surface of the ground.

PUBESCENT Softly hairy.

RACEME An unbranched racemose inflorescence.

RHOMBOIDAL Roughly diamond-shaped.

SAGITTATE Arrow-shaped.

SEPALS Green and leaf-like outer series of perianth segments situated directly behind the petals.

SERRATED Toothed like a saw.

SERRULATE Toothed like a saw.

SPADIX Fleshy spike-like flower head.

SPATHE Leaf-like sheath enveloping a spadix.

SPERMATOPHORE Collection of sperms.

STAMENS Male reproductive organ in a flowering plant.

STELLATE Star-shaped.

STIGMA The top of a pistil of a flower.

STOLONS Shoot from a plant—a runner or sucker.

THALLUS A simple plant organism which shows little or no differenciation into root, stem or leaf.

TRANSLUCENT Semi-transparent.

TRIFOLIATE Three-lobed leaves.

TRIPARTITE   Divided into three parts.

TRIQUETROUS   Having three acute angles.

TURBUCLE   Spherical or ovoid swelling.

TURION   Detachable winter buds.

UMBEL   A flower cluster in which the stalks arise from a common centre on the main stem.

VENTRAL   Belonging to the belly.

VIVIPAROUS   Live-bearing.

WHORL   A ring of leaves, flowers or petals.

PART ONE

THE POOL AND THE AQUARIUM

(1)

The Garden Pool

Whether it be in the serene calmness and mellow amber glow of a dewpond or the bubbling frothing fury of a mill-race, water has a peculiar fascination of its own which is shared by old and young alike. However, it is in the garden that it can be most readily appreciated; gently tumbling over rocks and splashing into a pool alive with the reds and yellows of goldfish, or in some sheltered nook supporting the broad verdant pads and brightly coloured waxy blooms of the waterlilies. In the water garden too every beauty is duplicated in the mirror-like surface of the pool. Here one can see again the azure sky above, watch the clouds and the birds as they pass overhead and note the long drawn shadows of neighbouring trees, pictured almost as clearly as when one looks directly at them.

Then—when we turn our attentions from the water itself to the surrounding ground a varied and unfamiliar range of plants presents itself. Marsh Marigold, Sweet Flag, Flowering Rush and Bog Arum with their feet in water throng the margins; while in the bog and on the banks that are slightly further removed, Gunnera, Cyperus, Primulas and Globe Flowers combine in forming a picture of unparalleled beauty.

Is it any wonder, therefore, that with so much beauty spread before us, that garden pools and water gardening are becoming so popular? Assuredly not. Since the advent of modern and relatively inexpensive materials for pool construction, the water garden has become a reality to all but the most impecunious of gardeners.

SITING THE POOL
The position in which a garden pool is placed in relation to other

major features—trees, walls, fences—is probably the most important factor influencing the ultimate success, or otherwise, of the venture. For apart from aesthetic considerations, those governing the welfare of plants and livestock must also be observed if a healthy balance is to be subsequently maintained. All aquatic plants prefer full uninterrupted sunlight and although some will tolerate shade these are usually the more sombre and less sophisticated subjects which the average gardener in the confines of a small artificial pool cannot spare the room to grow anyway. Fish, likewise, require as much sunlight as possible if they are to retain their brilliant colours and make satisfactory growth, although they do appreciate a shady corner in which to glide during the heat of a summer's day. But it follows that if a pool is placed in full sun, strong plant growth will result, which in turn will ensure that there is always plenty of surface shade available for the fish.

From the above, one can assume that any north-facing aspect or situation in the shade of trees is totally unsuitable for water gardening. On the other hand, however, a pool placed in the lea of a wall or fence with a southerly or westerly aspect has much to commend it, for here it will be protected during the winter from biting winds and yet not be shaded during the summer when sunlight is most important.

CHOOSING A DESIGN

The design one selects is purely a matter of taste, but for the end result to be really pleasing the choice should conform with certain basic principles.

Formal Design

In a formal garden the design should be symmetrical. A circle, oval, square, rectangle or an equally balanced complex of two or three of these is desirable and any fountain or ornament which is to be added, placed in such a position that when viewed from any angle the effect is one of equilibrium.

The surroundings are also very important with a formal pool, the material used being consistent and the lines created whether by a coping or paving, pronounced and severe. This is very important, for a formal pool with a path flanking one side, border another and lawn the remaining two, looks, if one may lapse into the East Anglian vernacular, like a 'pig's ear'; whereas one neatly surrounded by smooth paving stones is pleasing to the eye and has an air of cool cleanliness about it.

Formal pools are actually easier to design than either the informal or natural variety, for they can be sunken, raised or built up close to a wall without offending nature. However, planting has to be more carefully executed as a cluttered margin or crowded water surface give a messy appearance. The water surface in a formal layout should always have the full play of sunshine upon it and be only briefly punctuated by a clump of strategically placed water-lilies or possibly a cluster of the deliciously fragrant water haw-thorn. Indeed, in many cases, if the pool is left unplanted except for maybe a solitary clump of rushes and the required number of submerged oxygenating plants to keep the water fresh and clean, it is often more effective.

Informal Design
Informal pools of course are completely different and require margins filled with drifts of plants growing into one another in tangled profusion if they are to appear at all natural. Surface design is also a different matter, for it should be remembered that nature abhors a straight line and an informal garden is going along with mother nature—whereas a formal design is in strict con-tradiction of nature's intentions. However, it does not follow that because straight lines are undesirable that other fussy and irregular niches and contortions are any more acceptable. A pool of an informal kind should always be designed on a mathematical basis with sweeping curves and arcs with definite radii and not cluttered by severe or eccentric lines.

The immediate surroundings, unlike those of a formal scheme, should not be conspicuous; the harshness of concrete or fibre-glass being disguised by creeping plants such as Lysimachia or Herniaria, or else grassed right up to the edge. If a rock garden is being incorporated in the scheme, rocks can be introduced and brought down to the pool-side, or even right into the water with charming effect.

Internal Design

Having decided upon surface design and the incorporation of a water feature into the landscape, it is time to consider the internal design. Adequate provision should always be made so the housing of different types of aquatic plants and depths of water are compatible with the kind of ornamental fish it is envisaged keeping. Marginal plants—rushes, reeds, irises, etc.—require shallow water in which to grow and are usually grouped around the sides of the pool on shelves. These shelves are generally about nine inches deep —allowing for six inches of soil and a three inch covering of water —and sufficiently wide to accommodate planting containers. Water-lilies need much deeper water and should have a specially allocated place to suit their particular requirements.

Before deciding upon this, it is advisable to consult a good catalogue and select the varieties to be grown and then discover the optimum depth at which they will do best before constructing or purchasing a pool. However, if one is undecided, a good depth to allow is between fifteen and eighteen inches, as most of the popular and colourful kinds can be adequately accommodated in this.

Likewise, if any very fancy ornamental fish are to be kept— fantails, black moors, telescopes—a suitable depth of water in which they can overwinter should be provided. Again fifteen to eighteen inches is adequate, but for common goldfish and shubun-kins this can be reduced to nine or twelve inches without them coming to any harm.

TYPES OF CONSTRUCTION

Modern materials have taken much of the hard work out of pool construction. Gone are the days of puddled clay and gault, when one used to have to line the excavation with soot to prevent earth-worms from poking holes through the carefully laid finish, and hoses had to be kept at the ready on warm summer days to spray the walls where pool and lawn met to prevent cracking. But it would be a fallacy to suggest that building a pool is anything less than a muscle-toning exercise, for even with all today's improved aids few gardeners can afford to dig the initial hole with anything other than a spade and their own sweat and toil. However, once the excavation is complete the wide range of materials available will enable the would-be pool owner to choose a method of construction compatible with depth of pocket and strength of back.

Pool Liners
Pool liners are currently the most popular form of construction, for they are usually comparatively cheap and will suit any fanciful shape the gardener may care to design. They consist simply of a sheet of heavy gauge polythene or rubber material which is placed in the hole and moulded to the contours of the excavation by the weight of water within and then secured at the top by rocks or paving slabs.

Selecting a suitable liner often presents the beginner with considerable problems, for he will see that prices vary widely for products which appear on the surface to be almost identical.

The lower price range are usually of 500 gauge polythene in a sky blue colour and made in three or four standard sizes. Obviously mass production of lines like these makes for cheapness and, coupled with the relative ease of present-day polythene manufacture, make a popular and fast selling product. However, I would not on the whole recommend the purchase of this kind of liner if any degree of permanency is required. Whilst it is true that with great care a pool of this material will last for upwards of ten years, it is more likely that it will bleach and perish between water level and ground level within three or four years and consequently spring a leak. The most useful purpose to which this kind of liner can be put is as a small hospital pool for sick fish or temporary accommodation for plants and fish whilst the main pool is being cleaned out.

The pool liners which occupy the medium range are often the best buy for the average gardener as they are durable enough to incorporate as a permanent feature and yet sufficiently inexpensive as to be within financial reach of the ordinary working man. They are invariably of a polyvinylchloride (P.V.C.) material and available in stone, blue, green or imitation pebble, and whilst many are manufactured to standard sizes, for an extra few pence it is often possible for them to be cut to sizes in accordance with the customer's wishes. Stone and blue are the most popular colours and I understand now that several enterprising manufacturers are producing liners with a stone finish on one side and lagoon blue on the other.

In the more expensive class are the rubber and reinforced P.V.C. liners. The rubber kind are extremely durable and correspondingly expensive. They are invariably of a black matt finish, but can be painted with a specially prepared paint in blue, stone or green. The quality P.V.C. types on the other hand are slightly cheaper and differ from their less expensive counterparts by being reinforced with a terylene 'webb'. Although visible, this does not detract from its appearance and makes for a much more durable product.

Having decided upon the type of liner to be employed, it is then necessary to calculate the size. This is done by measuring the length and breadth of the pool or, if it is of an irregular shape, the size of rectangle which will enclose the whole and then adding on each side the measurement of the deepest part of the pool and the length required to mould into any marginal shelves that are anticipated. A further nine inches or a foot should then be added to each side to allow for anchoring at the top.

Whatever kind of liner is used, the method of installation is more or less the same. It is helpful to spread those made from a polythene or P.V.C. material out in the sun for an hour or so before working so that they become more pliable and mould to the shape of the excavation more easily.

The first essential is to scour the hole for any sharp objects— stones, sticks, etc.—that are likely to puncture the liner. In gravelly soils or those where flints and similar sharp stones are prevalent it is advisable to place a thin layer of sand over the floor to act as a cushion and line the walls with thick wads of dampened newspaper to prevent any projections from ruining the liner.

As polythene liners have little elasticity they should be installed without water being added, allowing plenty of room for move-

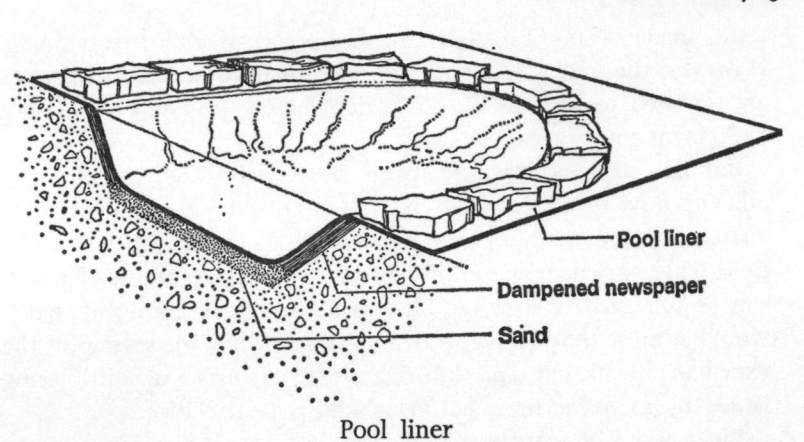

Pool liner

ment so that when it is introduced the liner moulds to the exact contours of the hole. P.V.C. and rubber liners can be stretched across the excavation and weighted down with paving slabs or stones. Water is then added and as the liner tightens, the anchoring weights on the ground are slowly released until the pool becomes full and the liner moulds to its exact shape. When the pool is full, and any unsightly wrinkles that might remain have been dealt with, the surplus material around the sides can be trimmed, allowing just sufficient to remain to enable the liner to be secured by paving slabs or rocks. The pool is then ready for immediate planting, for none of the specially designed pool liners contain any harmful elements likely to prove toxic to aquatic life.

Fibre-glass Pools
This latter quality is also responsible in no small measure for the increased popularity of pre-shaped pools of plastic or fibre-glass, for although the cost of these and concrete ones are comparable, one does not have the tedious task of scrubbing or soaking the surface in order to get rid of the effects of free lime before planting can begin. The cheaper brands of this kind of pool are usually vacuum moulded in a tough weather-resistant plastic and have a roughish undulating finish to simulate natural rock. Whilst being inexpensive and easily transportable, they do have the disadvantage of flexibility which can cause difficulty during installation, whereas

those made from fibre-glass are entirely rigid and free-standing. However, they are comparatively inexpensive and many beginners are tempted to try the plastic variety before investing in a more permanent job.

But for the experienced pond owner and the confident or affluent novice, a fibre-glass pool is a splendid investment. It is virtually indestructible and if treated with respect will last a life-time. There are dozens of different shapes and sizes, most of which can be obtained in a stone, blue, white or green colouring, and I would suggest that a prospective customer sends for several of the excellent illustrated and informative catalogues currently being issued by manufacturers before making a final choice.

But a word of warning: pools that are described as 'rock pools' or 'fountain trays' are not suitable for plants or fish and although many gardeners are attracted by their comparative cheapness they should read the manufacturers' description carefully before purchasing. 'Rock pools' are those designed to sit near the summit of a rock garden and from which water tumbles down a cascade unit into a lower pool. They hold a very small volume of water and cannot sustain any aquatic life, save possibly that of a handful of water snails and a couple of oxygenating plants. 'Fountain trays' are also too shallow; these are the types of pool in which a fountain alone is stood or into which a gargoyle may spout. Owing to the turbulence of water created in this environment little of any significance can be grown and although ornamental fish would survive they would not be very happy.

Pre-shaped Pools

Installing a pre-shaped pool is not terribly difficult if one knows how to tackle the job properly. Unfortunately most people attempt to dig out a hole in the shape of the pool—a method doomed to failure. A more practical approach is to dig out a rectangle to enclose the entire outline of the pool. Then place the pool on a thin layer of sand and by means of bricks and similar materials level it up so that from side to side and end to end it is completely level and approximately an inch below the surface of the surrounding ground. The levelling ensures that when the pool is filled, the water lies evenly and does not drain to one corner and over on to the lawn. The idea of the pool being lower than ground level is so that when backfilling takes place the lifting of the pool—which is inevitable when soil is rammed evenly around it—is no more than can be comfortably camouflaged when the job is finished. In soils that are stony or heavy and in poor tilth it is better to back-fill with sand, gradually removing any supporting bricks as the filling replaces them. This should be rammed tightly around the pool as any air pockets behind it may give rise to subsidence in years to come.

Concrete Pools

Finally we come to concrete which, if laid properly, is in my opinion still the best form of construction. Not only can it be prepared in several colours, but can be formed into almost any shape imaginable. The excavation should be taken out six inches larger than the desired finished size, the soil firmed and the whole lined with polythene or building paper before operations commence. It is best if the concreting can be done in one day as there is then less likelihood of a leak occurring. If this proves to be impossible, then the edges of the first day's concreting should be 'roughed up' so that the next day's concrete mixes with it. No more than twenty-four hours should elapse between joining any one batch of concrete and another if the possibility of leaking is to be avoided.

Although mixing concrete is hard physical work, there is nothing complicated or mysterious about it. A good mixture consists of one part cement, two parts sand and four parts ¾-inch gravel measured out with a shovel or bucket. This is then mixed in its dry state until of a uniform greyish colour. If a waterproofing compound is to be added, it should be done at this stage.

Proprietary brands such as 'Medusa' and 'Pudlo' come in a powder form and should be mixed in with the aggregate strictly according to the manufacturers' instructions. Water is then added and mixing continued until the agglomeration is of a wet, yet stiff, nature. A good guide to its readiness is to place a shovel into the mixture and withdraw it in a series of jerks; if the ridges thus formed retain their formation, the concrete is ready for laying.

It should be spread evenly to a depth of four inches over the floor and, if the slope of the sides permits, up these as well. Wire netting can then be placed on the concrete and trapped between the base and final layers to act as reinforcement. The final layer of two inches is then laid and given a smooth finish with a plasterers' trowel. If the pool sides are vertical or very steep, formwork may have to be erected. This is usually of rough timber and held in place to form a mould for the walls. To reduce the risk of the concrete sticking to the timbers, they should, strictly speaking, be greased or limewashed, but one can usually get away with

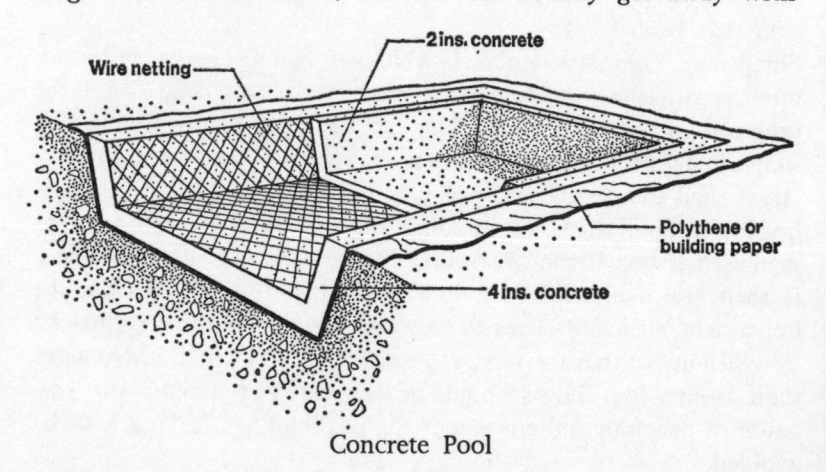

Concrete Pool

soaking the boards in water before pouring the concrete behind them.

When the pool is to be of an irregular shape and the harsh straightness of ordinary planks is undesirable, a successful result can usually be achieved by the careful use of plywood or other pliable material—suitably strengthened with ordinary timbers—and bent to the various contours that are desired.

When a coloured finish is required, the necessary ingredients should be added at the dry mix stage of the concrete used for the final layer. Pigments mixed in with the cement in any proportion up to ten per cent by weight of the same give a good even colouring. Red iron oxide provides a red colouring, chromium oxide a deep green, cobalt blue a blue, and manganese black, a black; whilst the use of Snowcrete cement and fine Derbyshire spar produces a really first class white finish.

A couple of hours after completion, when any lingering surface water from the concrete has soaked away, all the exposed areas of concrete should be covered with wet sacks, especially if the weather is warm and sunny. This prevents the concrete from drying too rapidly and hair cracks appearing. If the area to be covered is large, then regular spraying of the surface with water from a watering can with a fine rose attachment is to be recommended. Depending upon the weather, but after about five days, the concrete should have 'gone off' and be ready for treating prior to the introduction of plants and livestock.

As is well-known, concrete contains a substantial amount of free-lime which can be harmful in varying degrees to both plant and fish life. Leaving the pool to the mercy of the elements for about six months is the easiest method of preventing trouble occurring, but few gardeners are prepared to wait this long before introducing some kind of life. Many treatments are recommended by different authorities and include scrubbing the concrete with potassium permanganate, emptying and refilling the pool upwards of half a dozen times and many other laborious and dubious methods.

But from personal experience I would suggest filling the pool with water once and leaving it to stand for a week or ten days and then emptying. When the concrete has dried, an application of a neutralising agent, such as the well-known 'Silglaze' compound, should completely eliminate the chance of any trouble occurring.

It is also perhaps worth mentioning that in neutralising the lime, a product of this nature reacts to form silica—an insoluble compound—and thus seals the concrete by internal glazing. Rubber-based and liquid plastic paints also prevent free-lime from escaping when painted over the entire concrete surface, but in most cases it must be remembered that a special primer has to be applied first to prevent a chemical reaction between concrete and paint. These paints are available in several pleasing pastel shades and give a splendid finish to the pool, but unfortunately prove rather expensive when there are large areas to be covered.

FOUNTAINS AND WATERFALLS

Moving water is an asset in any garden, for apart from its obvious aesthetic qualities it is a valuable oxygenating aid, cooling the water on warm summer days when some of the more active species of ornamental fish may become distressed. It must be remembered, however, that when planning the siting of such a feature that few aquatic plants will tolerate moving water and therefore they should be positioned towards one end of the pool to allow a calm area in which waterlilies and similar subjects can be grown.

Manufacturers have produced a whole range of cascade units in shapes, sizes and colours to suit all tastes and full installation instructions are also provided. Some consist of a simple bowl with a lip over which the water trickles, whilst others come in sections of varying lengths and shapes and can be joined together to form quite complex arrangements. Installation is simple as they merely need siting securely in position and the delivery hose from the pump inserted into the uppermost one before being fully operational.

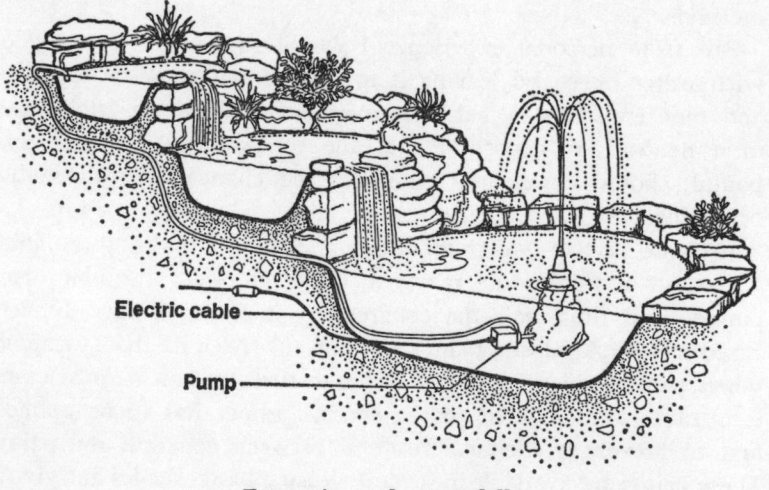

Electric cable

Pump

Fountain and waterfall

A fountain can sometimes be incorporated with a waterfall by the use of a two-way junction on the pump outlet, but in most cases the pump is not sufficiently powerful to produce the desired effect. A fountain alone is a much better proposition, and by the judicious use of jets with different numbers and arrangements of holes, some quite pleasing spray patterns can be obtained.

Apart from straightforward fountains, ornaments depicting mermaids, cherubs and other similar characters can be purchased, each designed to take a pump outlet so that water can spout from their mouths or any objects they may be holding.

The best arrangement that I have seen is with a fountain and series of bowls. Water is pumped up a tall central stem and falls into a small bowl. Beneath this are one or more bowls of increasingly greater sizes. The water from the fountain fills the first one which overflows into second, then into the third, and so on until it reaches the pool. This creates a magnificent effect, for as the water falls evenly from around each bowl it creates a thin swaying curtain, which in the midday sun is transformed into a glorious twisting kaleidoscope of colour.

The only disadvantage with this kind of feature is the excessive turbulence which occurs in the pool immediately beneath the fountain. However, this undesirable movement can be arrested if a ring of some kind is placed beneath the fountain in order to contain this movement, thus enabling waterlilies and other colourful aquatics to be grown in the relative calm of the outer perimeter.

Where space is very limited there is often insufficient room to accommodate a waterfall or display a fountain to full advantage and this is where 'masks' and gargoyles come into their own. These are usually imitation lead or stone ornaments depicting the faces of gnomes, cherubs or maybe even the head of a lion, and are flat on one side to enable them to be fixed to a wall. Water is pumped up into the mask and spews out from the mouth into the pool below. Again water turbulence presents a problem, but most aquatics will grow reasonably well if kept out of the direct flow of water.

But whether one decides upon flowing water or still, formality or informality, there remains one feature common to all which can give hours of added enjoyment and that is underwater lighting. It can be purchased in colours which vary from white and yellow, to red, blue or green, and is perfectly safe to use if handled sensibly. The manufacturers' instructions should be carefully followed when installing. The careful placing of spotlights to highlight waterfalls and fountains, or just the glassy stillness of the pool, soon transforms the garden into a glistening magical wonderland which the fortunate pond owner will find difficult to believe is his very own.

THE NATURAL WATER GARDEN

Although few people possess a garden blessed with natural water, where it is present one cannot do better than adapt it and work it generally into an informal landscape design. It is folly to attempt to convert such a natural asset into an artificial formal pool, since it can only be marginally improved upon aesthetically and then more by skilful planting than major structural alterations.

While it is true that a spring or rill can be used to fill a large pool and form small cascades through a rock garden with considerable effect it is wise to remember that although Nature can be a good servant it can equally be a bad master and that therefore any alterations anticipated must be carefully planned on paper before being executed. This is particularly true of a stream or brook which may be of minor local importance, for interfering with its flow in the most innocent of ways may lead to the inadvertent flooding of a neighbour's property or even one's own.

The only safe way the flow of such a stream may be checked or diverted slightly is by the addition of stepping stones. Strategically placed, these can create a calm area near either bank in which truly aquatic subjects may be grown more successfully than they might out in mid-stream. This particularly applies to waterlilies and other deep water plants which dislike turbulent or fast-flowing water. However, even when the current is too strong for this to be practicable, by planting Primulas, Mimulus, marsh marigolds and other waterside plants, its banks may be turned into a beautiful floral carpet for most of the year with the tumbling tinkling water a sparkling musical background.

Stepping Stones

Where a stream is wide or deep a bridge may be necessary to enable it to be crossed, or even when this is not essential a well-designed bridge in 'rustic' timber or local stone will make an attractive focal point. Stepping stones can also be used, but where these are intended for walking on rather than for diverting the flow of water, then it is important that they be reasonably level and have smooth, but not slippery, tops of sufficient area to accommodate a good size foot.

If local stone of such a type is difficult to come by, then they can be made cheaply and easily by mixing one part of cement to three parts of aggregate and pouring this into holes the size of the stones desired; these having been previously excavated in a piece of vacant ground. When the 'stones' have set, they can be excavated and placed in position, blending admirably into the general scene after being weathered for a few weeks.

Where local stone is plentiful, then that of a limestone nature should preferably be avoided as it is subject to water erosion while that of sandstone is quickly shaled by frost. All other kinds to my knowledge are quite suitable.

Bank Erosion

The gardens of riverside dwellers also suffer from frost damage and erosion, but of a different kind. Generally this occurs during winter when the water level has risen by maybe as much as three or four feet and plays havoc with the banks. Before or after a bend in the river this is a particularly common occurrence, for such bends divert the current's main flow from the centre and lead to erosion by scouring or by undermining the base of the bank so that the top subsides. Sheet erosion of the top soil also occurs but not only near the bends and this has to be combated by protecting the banks.

Several kinds of material have at various times been used for this work, but wood and steel are the most useful. Concrete should never be contemplated for, apart from being displeasing to the eye, it is a rigid material and incapable of withstanding the often opposing pressures of land and water. Wood is the most economical and easiest to work with, and the clever gardener can often, by driving piles and boards into the river near the mud banks, reclaim a considerable stretch of mud from the river. If this can be supplemented with soil and raised well above the water's edge to form a new bank it can then be planted with all manner of gorgeous moisture-loving plants.

Moisture-loving is the operative word, for a river, while being an excellent summer feature in normal weather, can become a terror in winter or after prolonged rainy spells, submerging plants for several days at a time. It is also wise to consider the proximity of the garden to the coast, for a river within a short distance of the sea comes very much under the influence of the tides and the effects of salt water, and a planting scheme has to be devised to cope with these factors.

THE BOG GARDEN

The bog garden is a natural extension of the pool in which moisture-loving plants can be grown. These in the main are border plants of the usual herbaceous nature which, although needing plenty of moisture to grow prolifically, cannot tolerate standing water. Under ordinary border conditions they often become stunted and their leaves burned at the edges because they are too dry, so the only place in which they can be grown properly is a bog garden. If situated adjacent to a pool they amply repay the trouble taken over constructing a marshy area by masking the pool edge and providing a pleasing background for the true aquatics.

Constructing a bog garden is not too difficult when in conjunction with a pool, but its development should be envisaged when the pool and its immediate surroundings are planned—preferably long before the pool is actually constructed. If the pool is to be made with a liner there is no difficulty in construction, for all that need be done is order the liner larger than required for the pool and incorporate it at the edge as if it were a spreading shallow pool about a foot deep. A retaining wall of loose bricks or stones should be spread across the border of the pool proper and the bog garden; the latter should be filled with a mixture of equal parts coarse peat and soil and laid over a layer of gravel. This gives a moisture

A formal pool. The design is symmetrical and the pool placed in such a position that when viewed from any angle the effect is one of equilibrium.

An informal pool. The margins are clothed with plants to give a natural appearance.

Tangled informality in a small pool.

Nymphaea Marliacea Chromatella, a medium-growing soft yellow waterlily.

retentive medium, but allows excess water to drain from the roots. Water from the pool moistens the soil through the barrier, the soil surface being an inch or so above the mean water level.

If the pool is to be of concrete, a similar construction in that material can be made. However, if a plastic or fibre-glass pool is used a small independent polythene-lined bog garden will have to be constructed in a similar manner to that described earlier. However, no matter what form the construction takes there are two points to remember when making such a garden and they are that the soil be moisture retentive and yet at the same time drainage must be provided.

Plants

The choice of plants for a bog garden is legion, so wide in fact that nothing but an encyclopaedia of bog plants could do justice to describing the wealth of beautiful plants that are available for effective grouping.

The tawny orange and rich yellow shades of the many Hemerocallis hybrids and the glorious crimsons, pinks and whites of the modern Astilbes coupled with the guardsman-like spires of the Aconitums fill the bog garden with colour throughout the summer. Early autumn brings the sulphurous pendant blooms of *Primula florindae* and the vivid scarlets of the perennial Lobelias, preceded by *Primula sikkimensis* and the deep-coloured Trollius which provide a similar striking contrast in the spring. A group of *Aruncus sylvester* with tall feathery plumes of creamy-white flowers furnished at the base with the cream and green variegated foliage of the Hostas or the cabbage-green leaves of the larger varieties would look magnificent.

In the smaller bog garden *Primula farinosa* can be grown with its mealy foliage and crowded umbels of soft rose flowers, while the flowering period can be much extended by planting the delightful silvery-white flowering *Parnassia palustris*. Indeed, with the many varieties available suitable for this kind of garden it is possible to have all manner of flower and foliage combinations and not only in spring and summer, but throughout the twelve months of the year.

(2)

Pool Management

THE POOL IN SPRING AND SUMMER

Although the pool is initially a time-consuming feature of the garden, once established its maintenance is relatively simple and undemanding. Routine care consists of keeping an eye open for pests and diseases; lifting and dividing waterlilies every third or fourth year and marginal plants alternate years. Feeding is also important, especially for Nymphaeas, as in common with many terrestrial plants they are gross feeders.

Fertilisers

Unfortunately, difficulty is often experienced in getting fertiliser down to the roots without lifting and replanting in fresh compost or considerably fouling the water. A certain degree of success can be achieved, however, by making 'bonemeal pills' which are dropped in the water alongside the plants. These are made with a handful of coarse bonemeal with sufficient wet clay to bind them together. Where plants are growing in baskets, these 'pills' can be pushed into the soil next to the roots. The frequency with which this operation should be carried out will vary greatly according to the variety and compost, but its need will be apparent when the leaves of the plant become yellowish and get progressively smaller and the blooms are of poor colour, with fewer petals and appear to be more or less abortive.

Marginal plants can also benefit from this treatment, but it should not be provided for those of a rampant or marginally uncontrollable nature—particularly Typha, Phragmites and Scirpus. Floating and submerged oxygenating subjects gain most of their nourishment directly from the water, so feeding of this kind for them is both wasteful and undesirable.

Feeding Fish

Feeding fish may be likened in many ways to that of plants, for not all species have the same requirements and overfeeding can be both wasteful and in a small pool dangerous, as any uneaten food will decompose and pollute the water.

There are basically three different forms in which one can obtain a completely balanced fish food. The conventional or crumb food, usually in a multitude of colours from the whites and ochres to red and vivid yellow, flaked foods which are also multicoloured, but take the form of thin tissues of flakes akin to a much refined version of breakfast cereal, and the floating pellet kind which are dark brownish in colour and about a quarter of an inch long.

All have their advocates and all to varying degrees their advantages and disadvantages. Both pellet and flake foods float for a considerable length of time and allow one to observe the fish feeding more than might be the case with the conventional crumb varieties. However, on windy days the flaked food often blows away or into a corner of the pool amongst rushes and out of the reach of the fish. It does not really matter which form the food takes; fish do not object to being transferred from a crumb to a flake diet providing that they both satisfy their nutritional requirements.

Variety foods such as dried flies, daphnia and shredded shrimp can be interspersed with the staple diet and will be much appreciated by the fish. Live foods, when available during the summer months, provide a welcome change and are particularly useful for fish with digestive troubles. Live daphnia or water fleas, gnat larvae and mosquito larvae are ideal. Indeed, the former can be set up into a culture to provide a continuity of supply. If a tub or water butt containing soft water has an inch of soil added and then allowed to settle, and a net full of daphnia introduced to the water, proliferation will be so rapid that a decent supply can be netted and fed to the fish at least twice a week.

Feeding with dried packeted food depends upon the weather

and time of year as to the quantity used. But throughout the summer months a pinch of food for each fish on alternate days would seem quite satisfactory. Another guide is the speed at which the food is cleared up. Any that is left after twenty minutes should be removed and the rate of feeding reduced until a happy balance is achieved.

Algae Control
Apart from the nourishment of animal and plant life, the only other important factor for the pool owner to contend with is algae control. Aquatic algae occur in various forms, but notably free-floating and filamentous. The free-floating or yellow-green algae consist of some four hundred different species which live mainly in freshwater or occasionally on mud. They are generally about the size of a pin head and occur in their millions to create a green 'bloom' or pea soup effect. The filamentous algaes on the other hand appear as free-floating silkweed or spirogyra which can be dragged from the pond by the handful, or else in thick mats known as blanket or flannel weed. Other kinds like the so-called mermaid's hair cling to plants and baskets and often coat the walls of the pool.

Control of the free-floating kinds is relatively easy with an algaecide based on potassium permanganate, but it must be treated on a dull day when the water is not too warm, or else the pool will turn a thick cloudy yellow and have to be emptied. Filamentous algaes can be controlled with proprietary algaecides such as the renowned Algymicin P.L.L., but after treatment all dead algae must be removed to prevent deoxygenation of the water. Those with a scientific turn of mind, however, can control algae more cheaply and equally successfully with straight chemicals. Indeed, in large areas of water this is often the only economical way of doing so.

Copper sulphate is undoubtedly the best, for in small regular doses it can be safely used when fish are present. Where fish are not present it can be used at a greater strength, being harmless to all the higher plants while controlling the algae quickly and effectively. It might also be mentioned that under these conditions the stronger copper sulphate application is usually sufficient to control aquatic pests like caddis fly and will curtail waterlily root rot and fungal leaf spots.

For successful algae control where fish are present a concentration of 0.33 ppm introduced on alternate days over the period of a fortnight usually clears all algal growth. Treated in this manner the water seldom suffers oxygen depletion and the fish are not subjected to asphyxiation by the copper sulphate combining with their body mucus as is often the case with higher concentrations.

In very hard water this dosage may need to be slightly increased as copper sulphate unites with the carbonate of the calcium carbonate to form an insoluble precipitate of copper carbonate. It is essential therefore to test the pH of the water. The water temperature at the time of application should also be ascertained as this may have an effect upon the reaction, for it is likely that the unstable calcium bicarbonate normally found in tap water would leave a higher concentration of calcium carbonate in warmer weather, thereby reducing the effect of the copper sulphate. However, if there are no fish in the pond a dosage of 2 ppm will kill all the algae at one go.

Another algaecide which can be successfully used is sodium arsenite, but great care must be exercised in its use as it is not only toxic to higher forms of plant life but humans as well. Although undesirable in the eyes of many people owing to its very nature, when used at concentrations of between 1.7 ppm for suspended algae and 4.00 ppm for blanket weed and lower submerged plants, it does have the advantage of being harmless to fish.

Finally, one other chemical which should perhaps receive a mention here is formalin, but a great deal more needs to be known about its effect on various plants before its use can be given an unqualified recommendation. A solution of 1 part to 4,000 destroys free-floating algae and is definitely beneficial to cyprinid fish, but it induces several cultivars of Nymphaea into rapid growth with leaf stalks becoming extended by two or three feet, and in the case of the deep water aquatic *Nymphoides peltatum* destroys it completely.

No form of algae control is permanent, but the most stable is embraced by the theory of natural balance as will be outlined later.

Most of the controls detailed previously are useful in preventing algae growing in a new pool until the fish and plants become established, but in a pond that is entering its second or subsequent years their use only effects a temporary cure.

THE POOL IN AUTUMN AND WINTER

Preparing for winter is a very important task, but with most gardeners a sadly neglected one. The first essential is to clean up the marginal plants immediately the first autumn frosts have turned the foliage brown, removing any dead or decaying material likely to pollute the water.

Waterlilies may be allowed to die down of their own accord, but any yellow leaves with soft crumbling edges or black spreading blotches should be regarded with suspicion and immediately removed as this could well be a sign of a waterlily leaf spot. Many gardeners feel concern for their waterlilies during winter, but they need not fear, for as long as there is between nine inches and a foot of water over the crowns they will be perfectly all right. Small and pygmy varieties that may be growing in a shallow rock pool can have the water drained off and the crowns covered with a generous layer of old leaves or straw for winter protection. When the fear of sharp frosts has abated they can easily be restarted into growth by the addition of water.

Most floating plants disappear during the winter months by forming turions or winter buds which fall to the bottom of the pool, remaining there until the warm spring sunshine stirs them into growth again. If these are collected before they sink and placed in a bowl or jar of water in a cool airy place they will start into growth much earlier and can do much to combat troublesome algal growth that is almost invariably experienced in early spring, by providing much desired surface cover.

Fish in Winter

Fish should be prepared for their long vigil by judicious feeding with dried flies, ants eggs and other delicacies throughout September and October, only as much being given as they can comfortably clear up in twenty minutes. When the weather turns cold and the fish cease to be active, feeding should be stopped and not recommenced until they are seen darting about again in early spring. All popular types of pond fish can survive for several months during the winter without feeding, as their body processes slow down in much the same manner as a tree or shrub which becomes dormant. Likewise they can stand extreme cold, and will not be seen to suffer even if frozen solid in a layer of ice providing this enforced refrigeration does not last longer than a week or two.

Obviously ice presents the greatest problem to the pondkeeper, as not only does it trap toxic gases, but can exert tremendous pressures capable of cracking the most expertly laid concrete. The best way of preventing the latter occurring is by floating a piece of wood or a child's rubber ball on the water, so that ice will exert pressures against an object which is capable of expanding and contracting. If a pump is used in the pool during the summer, then this can be detached and an electric pool heater installed in its place. This consists of a heated brass rod with a polystyrene float and is perfectly safe to use, keeping an area of water clear of ice in the severest of weather.

Alternatively, in the event of a prolonged cold spell when one fears for the safety of the fish, a hole may be made in the ice by placing a pan of boiling water on the surface and allowing it to melt through. This will release any noxious gases and ensure that the fish are not subjected to the shattering shock waves which accompany a well-meaning person trying to break the ice with a pick or similar instrument.

PROPAGATING THE PLANTS

Although the average pool owner will not wish to propagate aquatic plants on anything like the same scale as he might bedding or vegetable plants it is, nevertheless, like fish breeding, an interesting and worthwhile pursuit for those with the inclination.

Waterlilies

It may come as a surprise to many to learn that only two varieties of hardy waterlily, *Nymphaea tetragona* and *N.* Pygmaea Alba, are commonly grown from seed in this country. For most of the hybrids grown today are infertile and even those that do set viable seed, take so long to come to maturity when grown in this way that it is not a method usually worthwhile contemplating.

The seeds of both *N. tetragona* and *N.* Pygmaea Alba form in greenish-white fruits which become submerged immediately the flowers fade. They reappear at the surface again some three weeks later and if not collected immediately will burst open and scatter their contents into the water. The pods should be gathered after they have been submerged for about ten days, detached with as much old flower stem as possible, and placed in a shallow dish of water so that when they ripen the seed will not be lost. When the fruits are ripe they exude a clear gelatinous substance in which the seeds are embodied. No attempt should be made to separate them from this protective coating, but the whole sticky mass sown intact.

Finely sieved, clean garden soil without the addition of any fertiliser is the best sowing medium and should be put in shallow clay seed pans. The seeds are sown in as near a manner as possible to that advocated for most terrestrial plants, the jelly being spread evenly over the surface of the compost with a pair of tweezers. A light covering of soil is given and the pans sprayed gently overhead from a watering can to settle the compost. They can then be stood in a bowl, aquarium or similar receptacle with the water just lapping over the surface of the compost and placed in a warm sunny position.

After three weeks or so the first seedlings appear. They have tiny translucent, more or less lanceolate, leaves and look like an aquatic form of liverwort. During this time, and indeed for the first six months of their lives, filamentous algaeas are likely to be troublesome by becoming entwined amongst the fragile juvenile foliage, but these are easily controlled by any proprietary algaecide. However it is essential to remove the destroyed remains of the algae or else fermentation will occur with subsequent rotting of the Nymphaea foliage. When the first two or three small floating leaves have come to the surface the plants can be pricked out. They should be lifted in clumps, washed thoroughly to remove all the soil, and then gently teased apart. A standard plastic seed tray or plastic half pots are the most useful containers in which to prick out the seedlings, which should then be immersed so that the compost is about an inch beneath the surface of the water. This level however, can be raised considerably as the growths lengthen and become much stronger. After six or seven months the plants begin to crowd one another, at which time they should be carefully lifted and moved to their permanent quarters.

Apart from the varieties previously mentioned, all other varieties of hardy Nymphaea can be propagated by 'eyes', and indeed in most cases this is the common commercial practice. 'Eyes' are tiny growing points which occur with varying frequency along the rootstocks of mature hardy waterlilies. In most cases they appear as smaller versions of the main growing point, each with its own juvenile foliage seeming ready to burst into active growth, although with *N. tuberosa* and its varieties they take the form of brittle rounded nodules which can be easily detached.

Parent plants are generally lifted during April and May and the 'eyes' removed with a sharp knife. The wounds of both 'eye' and rootstocks are dusted with powdered charcoal to prevent infection and the latter returned to the pool. The 'eyes' are then potted individually into thumb pots or plastic multipot trays in a good stiff loam compost and stood in a shallow container to which has been added sufficient water to cover the rims of the pots. If the 'eyes' are very small it is advisable to give them the added protection of a cold frame or greenhouse during the early stages of growth. As they grow, the water level should be raised and the plants potted into successively larger pots until a four inch size is attained, after which it can be safely assumed that they will be capable of holding their own in the outdoor pool.

Whether or not one wishes to increase one's stock of waterlilies, there comes a time when a plant just has to be divided. This is usually indicated by a preponderance of leafy growth in the centre of the clump, accompanied by a diminishing flower size, or complete lack of the same. With most varieties this condition occurs after being left undisturbed for three or four years, although some of the smaller hybrids, such as the Laydekeri types, may go for as long as six or seven years without needing attention. May is the best time to perform this operation, the plant being lifted, washed and any adult foliage removed at source.

It will be seen that the plant consists of a main rootstock from which several 'eyes' have grown to form sizeable 'branches' and it is these side growths that should be retained, cutting them from the parent with as much healthy young rootstock as possible. The thick bulky part of the original plant is generally of little use and should be discarded. But all the 'branches' can be planted individually to form new plants, providing of course that they each have a healthy terminal shoot.

Tropical waterlilies, unlike their hardy counterparts, can be successfully grown from seed, the procedure differing very little from that advocated earlier. Sow the seeds in pans of sandy compost and place in water that is maintained at a steady temperature of 75°-80°F. Once the first floating leaves have developed, the plants may be potted and kept at the same temperature in full sunlight for the winter months. I find it imperative to keep them actively growing during the first winter, or they will almost certainly rot whilst lying dormant in the damp compost. Collection of the tubers in the autumn is out of the question, for they are so minute as to need a hand lens to be able to see them.

Conversely, though surprisingly, it is almost impossible to over-winter the large tubers which many varieties of tropical water-lilies seem to make, but most of them will in fact form a tiny tuber, about the size of a chestnut, at the base of the main crown which can be successfully stored. Nocturnal varieties and hybrids derived from *N. colorata* bear masses of spawn, or small tubers, on the surface of the parent as well as beneath, and should receive similar treatment.

In the early spring the young tubers can be potted about two inches deep in a sandy compost, and the pots stood in water at a steady temperature of 70°F in a sunny position. After about two weeks the young leaves will start to appear. When the first true floating leaves have developed, locate with thumb and forefinger the stem-like growth connecting the young plant to the tuber. Follow this growth down and carefully pinch it off just above the tuber, removing the young plant with its roots intact, but leaving the tuber in its pot. The young plant should be immediately potted and placed in a heated aquarium with a temperature of 70°-75°F. In two or three weeks the original propagating tuber will send up another plant, which can also be removed and potted. This may be repeated for three or four times before the tuber is allowed to retain the final plant.

The viviparous or live bearing group of tropical waterlilies are the ones which bear young plants in the leaf sinus. The frequency of occurrence and strength of growth of these young plants varies greatly with locality; those varieties reproducing viviparously in the south of England, often not doing so in Scotland. But as light and daylength are believed to be major contributing factors in these differences, the gardener can do much to assist proliferation by giving several hours of extended daylight with an ordinary tungsten filament lamp.

As young plants on the leaves develop roots, they should be removed and potted individually in small pots of sandy compost, and then stood in water which is maintained at a temperature of 60°-65°F, potting them into progressively larger pots as the need arises. They will probably grow strongly throughout the first winter and may even flower, but one need not feel any concern, for this is merely a sign of well being.

One drawback to this method of propagation, however, is the preponderance of multi-headed plants which occur. They will generally have smaller flowers than the single headed forms raised from tubers and produce irregularly placed clumps of leaves on the surface of the water. Not much can be done to alleviate this condition once a plant has become well-established, but practically all viviparous waterlilies can be readily divided into single plants whilst in the formative period.

The young plants must be removed from their pots as soon as the clusters of terminal growths are discernible, and a knife used to cut sharply through the thickening tissues where the new tubers are forming. By doing this, several tiny plants with roots attached can be removed from each individual tuber, and then potted up and grown on in the usual manner.

Other Aquatic Plants

Unlike waterlilies, which are a very unusual and special case, all the other aquatic plants likely to be considered for cultivation are propagated by five more conventional methods—division, cuttings, turions, bulbils and seed. In the section listing the different kinds of plants suitable for various areas of the pool (p. 77), mention is made of the best method of propagating each species under its respective heading, therefore it is only left for me here to write in general terms about these methods of propagation.

Division, as may be expected, consists of dividing a plant into two or more portions each capable of an independent existence. In many varieties, such as Typha and Scirpus, which produce a creeping rootstock, this involves removing a length of root with terminal shoot attached and planting separately. Of course with Alisma, Caltha and Irises which grow in clumps, the divisions are more like small plants and are separated from the main plant by hand or with a trowel in a similar manner to that advocated for ordinary herbaceous border plants.

Many plants which are readily divisible, Mentha and Veronica particularly, always make better plants from cuttings. The cuttings or lengths of stem about three inches long, are removed from the parent plant in spring when it is just starting into rapid growth. If inserted in a tray or pot of sandy loam which is partially or completely submerged in water, rooting takes place within ten days or a fortnight and the young plants thus become independent entities. Plants of the two types mentioned above are better replaced by vigorous rooted cuttings each spring as they tend to become very straggly and unsightly.

Oxygenating plants are almost always propagated by cuttings. Indeed, when first introduced to the pool the chances are that they were merely a sprig of cuttings held together with a lead weight. On being planted in a tray or pot of soil roots are rapidly initiated.

Winter buds or turions are another means of propagation common to many oxygenating plants, and one in which the gardener need play little part. Many submerged plants form turions at the end of each stem. These fall to the bottom of the pool and, by virtue of the fact that each plant normally produces several stems each season and each stem produces one turion, the plant is reproduced quite steadily. Certain floating plants, notably Hydrocharis and Utricularia perform similarly, falling to the bottom of the pool for the winter months as dormant buds, but bobbing to the surface during spring in increasing quantities.

Some marginal plants have a similar habit, but produce underground bulbils or food storage organs. Sometimes, as in Sagittaria they are principally a means of successfully over-wintering, but with others like Butomus they are designed rather as an aid to proliferation. Collection of bulbils from suitable plants during early spring, and planting individually in pots for those of some size, or else in trays of mud for the diminutive kinds, provides a good start for the young plants. When well rooted, sprouted, and growing actively, they can be planted in their permanent quarters.

Seed, of course, provides the readiest means of propagation for a whole host of subjects, but generally only those that can be found naturally in the wild will come true to type. Garden varieties have to be propagated vegetatively if they are to retain their character, and some such as the double form of *Caltha palustris* do not set seed.

With most aquatic plants seed should be sown immediately it ripens and for subjects like Aponogeton, should not be allowed to leave the water before sowing. Others like Pontederia germinate better when green, while members of the Arum family—Calla, Lysichitum, and Orontium—grow better when well ripened. Most aquatics will germinate in a wet heavy loam compost, although varieties with floating foliage appreciate an inch or two of water over their crowns once through the soil. It is seldom advisable to submerge freshly sown seeds immediately as they are often very light and float right out of the compost, and it is also useful to cover the surface of the compost with a thin layer of silver sand to discourage growth of pernicious algae.

BREEDING FISH

Most pool owners like to try breeding a few fish, even if they have to give them away to friends when they have finished. However, for a considerable number of people, breeding has its serious aspect and in many cases the garden pool is not planted so much for the benefit of the human eye as for the well-being and proliferation of the fish.

All fish the pool-keeper is likely to have, with the notable exception of catfish, are of the Cyprinid or carp family. Therefore all, except the bitterling (see page 158), have similar requirements for their successful reproduction. Certain species, notably orfe and tench, seem loath to breed freely in captivity in this country and are best not attempted. However, all the species known collectively as carp and, of course, the common goldfish and its forms reproduce freely and many interbreed with one another.

Before attempting to breed fish it is essential to fulfil at least some of their environmental requirements. Where breeding is the main interest the pool should have a sizeable shallow area uncluttered by marginal plants, but thickly planted with submerged oxygenating subjects. This provides suitable conditions for the deposition of spawn and, if cleverly constructed, allows the area to be separated from the main pool, thereby preventing the parents from preying on their young.

The breeding season in this country lasts from April until August, the sexual urges of the fish being stimulated by the warmth and light intensity associated with spring and summer. Most goldfish are sexually mature in their second year, although adulthood is related more directly to size than age. Any goldfish three inches or more in length should be capable of reproduction.

Many people start fish breeding by purchasing one or two matched pairs of goldfish and, whilst this is to be recommended, it does not follow that the pair purchased will breed with one another if there are other sizeable fish in the pond. This is why exhibitors select the male and female they require and keep them separate from all their other stock until mating has taken place. Generally like breed with like, but hybrids in the carp family are common and those of similar shape and constitution do interbreed. However, the fact that they are in the same family does not necessarily mean that fish so diverse as tench and, for example mirror carp, will interbreed.

Choosing a pair either from a local retailer or from established stock is not difficult, when one knows what to look for. First of all where breeding is being taken seriously, colour and conformation should be the prime requirement and any scaling or other desirable feature also taken into account. Sexing fish in the spring is relatively easy. Body shape when viewed from above is oval or elliptical for the female, and slim and pencil-like for the male, the male being further enhanced by white pimple-like nuptial turbucles which are sprinkled liberally over his gill plates and often on top of his head. Females with over-distended bodies that look full of spawn should be regarded with suspicion if being purchased, as having been kept in restricted surroundings may suffer, or be suffering, from spawn binding. (See page 200)

Spawnings take place at any time during the breeding season, several occurring each year, but their frequency seems to be coupled more with water temperature and similar factors, although nobody is by any means certain. During spawning, the male fish chases the female around the pool and amongst the 'weeds', brushing and pushing furiously against her flanks. She then releases the spawn, trailing it in and amongst the stems and foliage of submerged plant life. The male releases his milt or sperm bearing fluid amongst the eggs which then become fertilised. When this has happened the adults should be separated from the area in which the spawn has been deposited, or else plants covered in spawn removed to an aquarium containing pond water. The use of the same water is most important as it will be of the same temperature and composition as that in the pool and consequently not injurious to the eggs.

Apart from natural spawning, there is an artificial method. This involves a process known as stripping which is particularly valuable when a special strain of fish is involved—show fish especially. Although the operation can be performed theoretically at any time during the breeding season, June and July are the ideal months, for there will be females in the pool that have not spawned and will clearly be seen to be ready to do so.

A chubby female should be carefully netted and examined. If the vent is distended and slightly reddened, then the fish will be in a ready condition for stripping. This involves holding the fish in wet hands and applying gentle pressure to the sides of the belly, progressing towards the vent, and over a flat bottomed dish containing a little water. If done confidently and rhythmically the eggs will cascade into the dish and can be easily distributed by moving the fish to and fro.

The male should then be secured in the same manner, care being taken during netting not to encourage premature emission of the milt by his jumping or thrashing about in the net. By gently stroking the flanks and belly, the milky-white milt will be extruded and can be spread evenly over the waiting eggs. The secret of successful stripping may be summed up as careful but firm handling, but not pinching or squeezing. The latter will certainly bring no results and can easily damage the fish.

When the milt and eggs are in the dish fertilisation takes place and, after twenty minutes or so, when the unsuccessful sperms have succumbed the eggs can be washed in clear lukewarm water. This renders them as clean as possible and discourages to some degree the incidence of fungal attack. They may be hatched in the dish with a little water, or else transferred to a well-furnished aquarium. After three or four days the fry will be seen to be developing. First of all they are difficult to see, resembling tiny pins in the water clinging to plants. However, after a couple of weeks they are recognisable as fish, sometimes transparent, sometimes bronze, but all eventually attaining their correct adult proportions and hues.

Few problems beset a pool-owner who would like to breed a couple of dozen fish. It is only when those of show standard are involved that trouble arises. Indeed, if goldfish and carp are placed in a pool, providing the sexes are reasonably evenly balanced, they will probably breed with some measure of success unintentionally without the pool-owner having to lift a finger.

(3)

The Indoor Pool and Aquarium

THE INDOOR POOL

One would be presumptuous to declare that the cultivation of tender aquatics in a greenhouse or conservatory is anything other than an expensive business. For not only has one the cost of constructing a building to surround the pool—although it is more likely that the reverse would be the case and the pool be constructed within an existing structure—but one has an argument with one's conscience as to whether the luxury of cultivating a few tropical waterlilies outweighs the economic advantages of growing the tomato and cucumber requirements of the household.

Heating is another expense, for to grow tropical aquatics such as Nymphaeas and Nelumbiums to anything like perfection, one must have a temperature of at least 60°-65°F in early spring, which during most seasons is the coldest part of the year. If, however, pockets are deep and ears well muffled to the grumblings of the conscience or indeed one's wife, then a most rewarding hobby can be undertaken in the cultivation of tender aquatics.

Pool construction follows the same principles as outlined earlier, but without the same worries as regards the elements, frost in particular, as in an outdoor venture. In fact, in a greenhouse or conservatory it is nice to have the pool somewhat raised, perhaps with a walled surround so that on a warm summer day one can sit on the edge and dabble the fingers in the tepid water as the fish glide and laze amongst the 'lily' pads. The proximity of life in such a pool to the observer is so close and the antics the various inhabitants perform such, that one is inclined to linger longer than intended. Indeed, the indoor pool is as great a time-waster as the television, but at the same time can be equally as educational.

For those less affluent, tub culture can be employed, almost any tender aquatic being grown satisfactorily this way. The exact method of culture is dealt with under the section dealing with tropical waterlilies, which are indeed the best plants for such containers. However, if the instructions given for their cultivation are followed with slight adaptations according to species, then the majority of tropical aquatics can be grown this way.

Apart from the purely tropical pool and the very obvious rustic outdoor kind, there is an intermediate that is so often overlooked, and that is the heated outdoor pool. Again one has to be 'well breeched' to cope with the finances—particularly the initial ones—of creating such a feature, but the result can be superb; witness the fabulous heated outdoor pool at the Royal Horticultural Society gardens at Wisley.

THE AQUARIUM

For many years now the aquarium and the keeping of both tropical and coldwater fish have been popular hobbies. Particularly so in recent times with the advent of tower block dwelling in which the normal kinds of pets are either prohibited or impractical to keep. This is understandable, for not only are fish easy to maintain, free generally from smell and able to be left for short periods of time without attention, but also in a well set-up tank create a living, moving picture of surprising beauty. It is not my intention here to dwell on all the advantages of the aquarist's hobby, or to explore it in any great depth, for it would take a book—a volume of considerable magnitude—to describe all the varieties of plants and fish available and their special requirements. It is rather to introduce the pool-owner to the possibilities extended by the aquarium, possibilities which are often triggered off simply by collecting a few goldfish fry from the pond in order to grow them on in safety, that this section is intended. In fact many pool-owners discovered their longing for a pond in the reverse manner having kept aquarium fish for a number of years and to them I apologise, although I hope they will be able to glean at least a morsel of beneficial information from the following pages.

Choosing and Equipping an Aquarium

The choice of an aquarium is almost, if not more important than the choice of fish or plants, for it must be remembered that apart from being pleasing to the eye it is also the permanent home of the fish. It should therefore be reasonably spacious and with as large a surface area as possible for the volume of water contained. An ill-chosen aquarium, no matter how attractive in appearance, will not be enhanced by its inmates if the design is such that the poor creatures are uncomfortable or distressed.

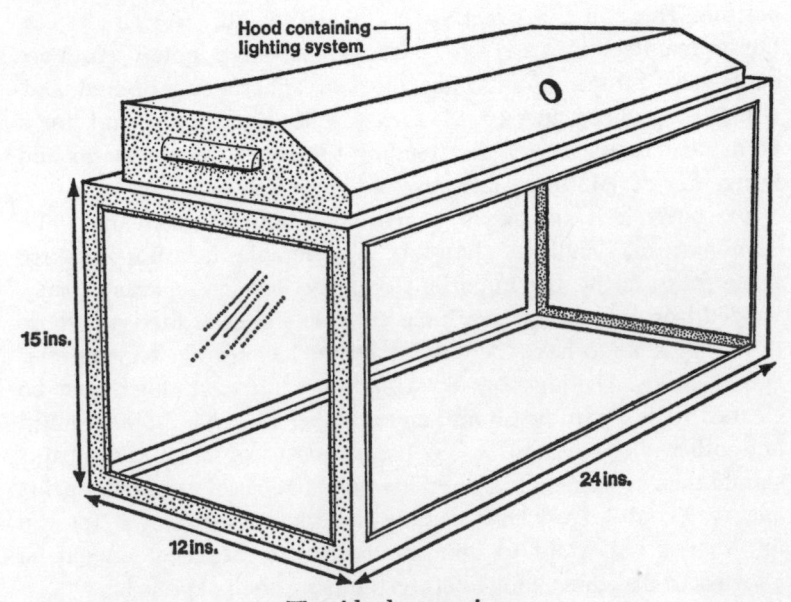

Hood containing lighting system

15 ins.

24 ins.

12 ins.

The ideal aquarium

The size one chooses is of little account and one will be governed to a certain extent by depth of pocket and space available, but for a good general show-piece aquarium I would hesitate to purchase one under 24 in. long and would prefer it to be 12 in. wide and 15 in. deep, or 15 in. wide and the same depth.

The material it is constructed of is a fairly important factor in making a final choice, although here again finance will figure prominently. The cheapest kinds are of plastic and formed in one piece, ranging in length from 12 in. to 4 ft and with matching hoods and bases of similar materials. They are ideal as beginners' tanks or reserve quarters for young or sick fish, being relatively inexpensive and for what they are, very good value. However, they are not ideal for tropical fish, as the injudicious use of the heater can melt part of the floor or wall. They are also very prone to scratches although, if not too deep, these can be removed with a proprietary metal polish such as Brasso.

Glass tanks are a similar proposition, by far the best buy being a metal or fibre-glass framed tank with traditional glass sides and bottom. These in the latest types of manufacture are almost certainly maintenance-free and, although of high initial cost, are extremely durable. Sometimes all-glass aquaria are offered and, while being cheap and useful, they are not the kind of tank for a permanent feature, the glass tending to distort the occupants and being very fragile incapable of standing rough handling.

Of course it is possible to construct a tank yourself and while economics may indicate that this is preferable, it is not a course to be followed by the impatient or heavy-handed aquarist. Ready welded iron frames are available from any decent sized pet shop, or it is possible to have them made by the local garage to your own specifications. Having secured a suitable frame, it must then be cleaned with a wire brush and emery paper to free it from rust and any other loose debris. A couple of coats of aluminium paint should then be applied followed by an undercoat of a good flat paint and two coats of an enamel paint of the colour chosen for the finish. It is important to mention here that each coat should be allowed to dry thoroughly before the next one is applied.

Glass may easily be obtained cut to size from any builders' merchant, but it is important that it be of the required thickness and weight for the use to which it is to be put. For example, in our 'ideal' tank which is 24 × 12 × 15, the base should be of quarter-inch wired plate, the ends of 32 oz. sheet and the front and back of 42 oz. sheet. The dimensions of each should be carefully measured, as the base is generally cut to size but with ⅛ in. to spare all round.

The front and back panels are next to be considered and their lengths will be the same as the base glass but to allow for the thickness of the base and the putty layers above and below they must be about ⅝ in. less than the internal frame height. Likewise the end pieces will be the same height as the front and back panels of glass, but will need to be about an inch shorter than the internal width of the aquarium frame.

Thus for our 'ideal' tank the dimensions will be: base 23½ in. × 11½ in.; front and back 23½ in. × 14½; and ends 11 in. × 14½.

The actual glazing is not difficult if a proper aquarium putty is used and if time and care is taken a leak-proof job can be easily executed. First of all, the putty should be spread evenly to the depth of about ¼ in. in the frame angles, making sure that there are no small air pockets. The glass must then be pressed firmly and evenly against the frame and any excess putty that extrudes around the edges trimmed off with a knife. It is important at this juncture to consider the order in which the glass is inserted. The base should be first, followed by the front and rear panels, and finally the two ends.

Having pressed the glass into position weights should be placed on the base and small wooden struts arranged to keep all the vertical panels in position. The aquarium must then be left for three or four days during which time a further coat of gloss paint may be applied to the exterior. The struts can then be removed and the aquarium filled with water.

No matter what type or size of aquarium is chosen, it will be necessary to provide a stand or similar suitable support. The angle iron types are probably the best as they can be painted to blend in with the tank or room decor; however, it is important that they be stood absolutely level or else a strain may be placed upon the frame and coupled with the vibrations of footfalls nearby, could lead to fracture of one or more glass panels.

With tropical aquaria in particular, a hood or cover is necessary, as this provides a means for fixing artificial lights, retains a certain amount of heat and prevents airborne dust from entering. This latter is also a good argument for attaching a hood to a cold-water aquarium, although it is by no means essential if the tank is positioned in the bedroom or study. Hoods are made of several materials, but more usually plastic or metal, and are designed so that a light can be incorporated, an aerator connected and food can be placed either through a small feeding hole in one corner, or else by lifting the entire lid which is securely hinged to the back. Some hoods have ventilation grilles in the top, whilst others are devoid of such features, but no matter what the design may be it is essential in a tropical tank to have artificial aeration and is beneficial in a cold-water aquarium where no other means of oxygenation is available.

Simple electric pumps costing little more than a couple of pounds coupled with a length of rubber or plastic tubing and an airstone to diffuse the air into a spray of fine bubbles through the water, are

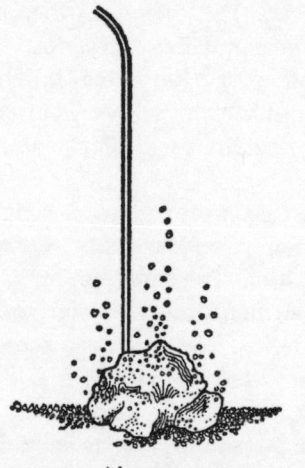

Airstone

readily available and easily installed. A filter of the conventional box shape or of the under gravel variety can also be worked in connection with an air pump and are a valuable aid in collecting waste matter in suspension in the water. The local aquatics dealer will be able to advise on the wide range available and the one to suit the purpose for which the tank is being used. If a filter is not used, ornaments of various kinds such as divers which bubble furiously, mussels which open and close periodically and all manner of gaudy plastic starfish and crustaceans can be attached to the air-line to diffuse the air. To my mind they are hideous, but for a large number of aquarists they hold a peculiar fascination.

Lighting in an aquarium is desirable, especially for the winter months when plant growth is slow. Most aquarium hoods have provision for one or two strip lights and I find two thirty watt clear lamps burning for six or seven hours each day sufficient for the needs of both plants and fish. Some enterprising manufacturers are now producing similar tubes in different colours and although comparatively expensive can in subtle blue and pink shades give a spectacular effect to a tropical tank.

Heating, of course, is unnecessary and undesirable in a cold-water aquarium, but is an essential for the tropical tank. Electrical

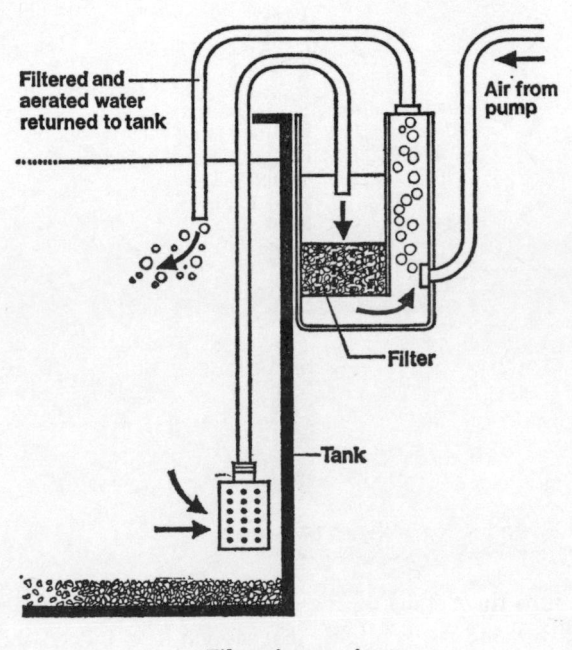

Filtration unit

immersion heaters worked in conjunction with a thermostat are the most satisfactory method of heating and to raise the temperature of the water to the optimum 75°F required in an ordinary community tank, one of seventy-five watts rating will be needed for our 'ideal' aquarium. For those of greater size two heaters are needed, one at each end, in order to distribute the heat evenly.

A reliable thermostat makes for economical use of electricity and also enables one to use with safety a heater of greater wattage than necessary. It also follows that if the water is to be heated an accurate thermometer becomes essential. These take different forms; some are of the slim glass tube type and attached to the side panels by means of a rubber sucker, whilst others float, weighted at the base by a small quantity of lead shot, However, it is the slightly more sophisticated, and need I add more expensive, type with a round dial and rubber suction ring which adheres to the glass that I prefer.

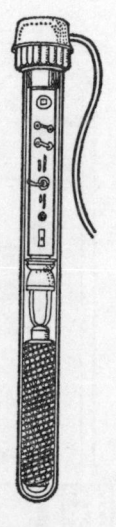

Thermostat

To go into the details of the different kinds of equipment on the market is beyond the scope of this section, and indeed the scope of this book. However, several ample tomes of wonderful value giving the fullest information on every aspect of the hobby are readily available and certainly a good investment for the would-be aquarist. Most dealers in aquatic accessories are helpful in advising the beginner and showing him the items he requires and making suggestions as to the products best suited to his needs. I have found this particularly true of the small establishment where the proprietor is often the assistant, tea boy and, what is most important, something of a hobbyist himself.

Setting up an Aquarium
Having decided upon the branch of the hobby to be pursued and with all the essential equipment to hand, it now falls upon the aquarist to perform the pleasurable task of setting up and land-scaping the tank. The background is the first to be decided, for upon this the whole theme of the tank depends. A plain paper backing of black, mauve or deep blue is preferred by some, while others plump for elaborate underwater seascapes with grottos, caves and exotic-looking fishes. These are purchased like wallpaper on a continuous roll and the dealer will cut off the desired length. This is then stuck to the back of the tank in the same manner as a shopkeeper might stick a poster to his window.

The next stage is to spread gravel and sand evenly over the floor of the tank, covering a layer of finely sieved peat which should be provided for the plants to root into. This also acidifies the water to the benefit, particularly, of tropical fish. Fine silver sand to the depth of ¾ in. is an ideal first covering to the peat, followed by a further ½ in. of washed shingle or multi-coloured dyed grit which is sold specifically as aquarium gravel. Coloured glass chips which have been sand blasted to smooth off the sharp edges are sold for the same purpose and some aquarists even cover the sand with a layer of children's marbles with extraordinary effect. Some fish, such as catfish and loach, are not really at home with gravel in their tanks, and for these an additional depth of soft sand is advisable. I find one of the best sands to use is that prepared for cage birds and even if this has 'tonic grit added' it appears not to be harmful to fish.

The growing medium prepared and undulations created to give an illusion of an aquatic terrain, one can now introduce ornaments or rockwork. As with gnomes fishing around a garden pool, I have an intense dislike for gaudy arches, shipwrecks, treasure chests, mermaids and all the other paraphernalia that commerce has introduced. Well-placed natural rocks or artificial rocks and cliffs of natural appearance do much to enhance an underwater picture.

However, as when constructing a rock garden, it is essential in the aquarium to be sure that the strata, should such exist, be placed in the same plane. Violent clashes of colour, such as white spar with red Mendip stone, or black Devon rock with red or green granite, must be avoided.

Water can be added as soon as construction is complete. This can come from several sources but by far the safest is direct from the tap. Although possessing a high chlorine level, this is rapidly dissipated, particularly in a warm atmosphere. Filtering the water through activated carbon or treating with an anti-chlorine concentrate has the same effect. Rain water can be used if one knows how it has been collected. In any case, it is only wise to use that from a country area as rain water in a town often has a high concentration of dissolved salts present.

The pH level, or acidity of the water, is often quoted in articles relating to different species of fish, but unless the values are at the extreme ends of the scale, for the beginner this factor can be safely ignored.

The actual introduction of water should not be violent, for a jug, bowl, or bucket upended over the carefully laid landscape will leave it in ruins. The easiest and safest way of filling the tank is to fill a bucket with water and siphon it out onto a sheet of polythene spread over the gravel, by means of a narrow rubber tube. By doing this, unnecessary disturbance of the terrain is avoided and, as the level of the water rises, so the bag is lifted until it reaches the top of the tank and is then easily removed. The aquarium is now ready for planting.

PART TWO

PLANTS AND PLANTING

(4)

Plants for the Pool

Water gardening is unlike any other branch of horticulture, for when planting a pool one is creating a whole new world in which plants, fish, and snails rely upon one another to provide the basic requirements necessary for their continued existence. Submerged oxygenating plants replace the oxygen that has been lost to respiration and compete with slimes, algae and other primitive forms of plant life which turn the water thick and green, by using up all the available mineral salts and thereby gradually starving them out of existence. Floating plants make life intolerable for any green water-discolouring algae that try to dwell beneath them. Waterlilies and marginal plants, although of no great importance in creating a balance, provide the necessary colour to make the pool a continual source of pleasure and delight.

From the visual point of view, it is beyond all reasonable question that waterlilies should occupy by far the largest area of the available water surface. However, I would enter a strong plea for reasonable representation of the various other beautiful flowering and foliage plants that do so much to complete the perfect picture. The lovely double form of the Japanese arrowhead, with impressive foliage and white flowers clustered in rounded heads; the stately pickerel, its spikes of bright blue flowers associating with luxuriant leaves; the greater spearwort bearing its giant buttercup flowers and the beautiful and most desirable pink flowered *Butomus umbellatus*. *Iris laevigata* is equally happy in shallow water or at the edge of the pool, where it may have as companions the fascinating bog bean, Mimulus in great variety, the magnificent skunk cabbages, hardy Lobelias and dozens of other delightful plants. Indeed, the pool and its immediate vicinity give enormous opportunity to the skilful planter.

WATERLILIES

Although there are very few species of the true waterlilies (Nymphaea) worthy of cultivation, hybridisers, notably Marliac of France and Dreer of America, have bequeathed to us a wealth of outstanding garden varieties for all depths of water and in almost every colour imaginable. At present blue is the only colour not available to the gardener, but as there are several blue flowering tropical species in cultivation the possibility of raising a blue variety sufficiently tough to withstand the rigours of our winter climate is not as remote as it may seem.

All the hardy waterlilies bloom during the day, opening at about noon and closing as the sun begins to set. The flowers last for up to five consecutive days in warm sunny weather, but if subjected to several hours of rain will often become water-logged or 'balled' and fail to re-open.

Containers

There are basically two methods of growing waterlilies. One is to cover the pool floor with six inches or so of prepared compost and plant directly into this, or else use some kind of container—a pot, box or basket. Most gardeners prefer the latter method, for then the plants can be easily removed for inspection or division, or in the event of the pool needing to be cleaned out. Specially manufactured waterlily baskets are infinitely superior to any other kind of receptacle one may contemplate using and are readily available from most horticultural sundriesmen. Usually they are of a heavy gauge rigid polythene or plastic material and of a design that will not easily become unbalanced and topple over in the water. Occasionally, one may come across an old-fashioned lily basket or wooden planting crate and these will be just as suitable, although not quite as durable.

Compost

Contrary to popular belief, there is nothing mysterious or wonderful about the compost used for planting waterlilies. Good clean garden soil from land that has not recently been dressed with artificial fertiliser is the main constituent. It should be thoroughly sieved and care taken to remove twigs, weeds, pieces of turf, old leaves or indeed anything likely to decompose and foul the water. On no account should soil be collected from wet, low-lying ground, or natural ponds or streams, as this will often contain the seeds of pernicious water weeds which may be difficult to eradicate at a later date.

Having prepared the soil, a little coarse bonemeal may be added. I generally allow a handful for each basket to be planted and mix it really thoroughly into the compost. A coarse grade of hoof and horn meal or similar slow-acting nitrogenous fertiliser may be used instead, but only sparingly, and not in the popular powdered form, as this will usually cloud the water and may even prove to be toxic to the fish.

Many old gardening books recommend the liberal use of rotted farmyard manure or cow dung in waterlily composts. But I have found this to be dangerous practice, for unless one exercises great care in ensuring that it does not come into direct contact with the water, pollution is likely to occur. If it is felt that one's soil lacks a certain amount of 'body' and would benefit from the addition of some organic matter, I have found that the turning and mixing of the soil with well-rotted manure at regular intervals over a period of twelve months will provide an admirable planting medium for waterlilies. But to do this one has to have considerable foresight and a tremendous amount of patience.

Planting

Planting time can usually be taken as extending from late April until mid-August and should be carried out in the case of a new pool whilst it is still empty. The compost, prior to planting, should be made to such a consistency that when squeezed in the hand it binds together, yet is not so wet as to allow water to ooze out through the fingers.

Before attempting to plant, the rootstock of the waterlily involved should be carefully studied. Those of the *N. odorata* and

N. tuberosa varieties have long, white, fleshy rhizomes and should be set horizontally about an inch below the surface of the compost with just the crown exposed. The Marliacea and Laydekeri hybrids, and many intermediate varieties, have bulky log-like rootstocks with fibrous roots arranged like a ruff, immediately beneath the crown. These are planted vertically, or at a slight angle, with the crown protruding above the planting medium.

It is advisable before planting to remove all the adult leaves at the point where they emerge from the crown. This may seem drastic, but they would in all probability die anyway and when planted with the foliage intact, they often act as floats giving the plant buoyancy and lifting it right out of the basket. Similarly, the fibrous roots should be cut back to the rootstock and any dead or decaying area of the rhizome pared back with a knife to live tissue and dressed with powdered charcoal to help seal the wound. If a rootstock takes on a gelatinous appearance and is evil-smelling, avoid contact with other sound varieties, for this is a certain indication of infection with the waterlily root rot.

When planting, be sure that the compost is packed as tightly as possible in the container, for it will be full of air spaces, and will decrease considerably in volume as the water drives the air out. I have often seen the rootstocks of newly planted waterlilies left completely exposed following this sinking effect and, in many cases where their roots have not had a chance to penetrate the compost, the whole plant has come floating to the surface. Watering newly planted lilies like pot plants, prior to placing in their permanent quarters, usually helps to settle the compost and alleviates much of this trouble. A layer of washed shingle about an inch deep should be spread over the surface of the planting medium to discourage fish from nosing in the compost and clouding the water. But this should not be collected from the sea-shore, as it will have a high salt content which may prove detrimental to the other inhabitants of the pool.

Place the planted baskets in position in the pool and run in enough water to cover their crowns. Then as the young foliage appears gradually raise the level of the water. Never plunge the waterlilies directly into two or three feet of cold water unless

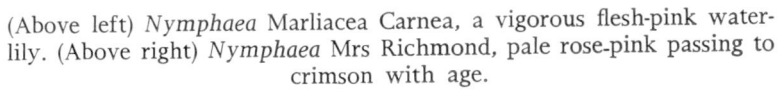

(Above left) *Nymphaea* Marliacea Carnea, a vigorous flesh-pink water-lily. (Above right) *Nymphaea* Mrs Richmond, pale rose-pink passing to crimson with age.

Nymphaea Gladstoniana, with exceptionally large pure white blooms.

Aponogeton distachyus, the sweet-scented Water Hawthorn.

Nymphoides peltata (syn. *Villarsia nymphaeoides*), the Water Fringe.

absolutely necessary, for they have already suffered a considerable shock by being moved and defoliated whilst in active growth. If you are merely adding to your plant collection, or replacing a dead or overgrown waterlily in an existing pond, then this procedure can be reversed, the basket being stood on a pile of bricks and lowered gradually one by one as the growths lengthen.

When planting into compost on the pool floor all the same general rules apply, but perhaps one small hint may not come amiss and that concerns the filling with water of this type of pool. It follows that if a hosepipe is placed directly into the pool and turned on, the water will stir up the soil and become cloudy, but by placing the end of the hosepipe on a large sheet of polythene and allowing the water to trickle over the edges this is prevented. As the water level rises, the polythene is lifted and trapped against the end of the hosepipe, which, if the sheet is large enough, will also be gradually raised until the water is at the desired level.

Planting in Natural Ponds
Now just a word for those few gardeners who are fortunate enough to possess natural ponds, for in these circumstances entirely different planting methods have to be adopted. These often conflict with the advice given previously and are usually only effective because stronger and more vigorous growing varieties are used in these situations.

Obviously it is impractical to empty such a pond and plants therefore have to be planted through the water. The best method is to plant them in prepared compost on squares of hessian, whose four corners are then lifted and tied just beneath the crowns. These 'packages' can then be gently placed in the water and allowed to sink to the bottom. The hessian will eventually rot, by which time the plants will be well-established in the compost and may even have penetrated the surrounding mud on the pool floor. In large expanses of water where groups of waterlilies are required, they can be planted two or three together in a wooden orange box, taken out to their positions in a boat and lowered over the side.

Positioning

The actual positioning of waterlilies in a pool is dependent upon several factors. Firstly the depth of water available, which in turn determines within limits the varieties which can be safely grown; also the presence of moving water, which will cut down considerably the number of plants which can be accommodated for few varieties will tolerate even the slightest movement in the water and therefore are totally unsuitable for streams, or pools where a fountain is constantly playing. Sunlight is another important consideration and plants should be placed in positions where they will receive the maximum number of unbroken hours. Where none, or only a few, of these necessary conditions exist, then it is advisable to look at the possibilities of substituting with varieties of Nuphar as they will tolerate almost everything that the Nymphaeas abhor.

Varieties

There are many different kinds from which to choose—over 190 garden varieties alone—but many of these differ only slightly from one another and some are not considered by nurserymen to be worth growing, or are so slow in reproducing that they are not viable commercial propositions. Therefore I have thought it advisable to restrict my selection to those that are currently available from most specialist nurseries.

They are not arranged in any specific botanical order as knowledge regarding their derivation is very sparse. Alphabetical order is the principal system involved, although hybrids known to have been directly derived from a species will be located as such under the respective species heading. The figures in brackets following a description refer to the depths of water in which each variety may be successfully grown.

The Waterlily Species and their Varieties

Nymphaea alba: Common white waterlily. This is a handsome plant for the larger pool, where once established it will produce showy snow white blossoms some three or four inches across that float like glistening chalices amidst the large and resplendent dark green leaves. A double variety called 'Plenissima' is occasionally offered and is infinitely superior to the common form. (Up to 6 ft.)

N. candida: A tough and resilient species for shallow water. Throughout the summer this little fellow produces a succession of small white, cup-shaped blooms with golden stamens and crimson stigmas. Many forms are known to exist, but only the Russian *var. wenzelii*, with unusual star shaped flowers, is at all common, and then only in old and well established gardens. (1-1½ ft.)

N. caroliniana: A very fragrant soft pink variety which may be a little shy in flowering for the first twelve months after planting. Many authorities consider this to be a natural hybrid between *N. odorata var. rosea* and *N. tuberosa*; it certainly has the excellent qualities of both. Three cultivars from this are commonly available; the pure white 'Nivea', salmon pink 'Perfecta' and the rose pink 'Rosea'. (1-1½ ft.)

N. fennica: This is a small growing species for a cool and partially shaded situation in the shallows of the pool or on the marginal shelf. The curious white star-like blossoms are sprinkled liberally amongst delicate soft green pads. (1 ft.)

N. nitida: An unusual and extremely hardy miniature which was introduced from Siberia over 150 years ago and bears tiny white, scentless cup-shaped flowers during June and July. (1 ft.)

N. odorata: Sweet Scented Waterlily. An excellent species for the small or medium sized pool. Fragrant white flowers up to six inches in diameter borne amongst handsome pea-green leaves which are purplish when young, and usually remain so beneath throughout the season. *Nymphaea odorata* and all its many varieties and hybrids have very distinctive circular leaves that makes them instantly recognisable from any other species. Most forms of the species are in cultivation and respond well to pool culture. The diminutive *odorata var. minor*, a splendid miniature variety from the shallow bogs of New Jersey, is probably the best known. This has small fragrant, star-shaped blooms and soft green leaves and is equally at home in a sink garden or pool. A version of this with pink reverses to the petals, *odorata var. minor floribus roseis*, may occasionally be encountered and is a further improvement on the type. Another popular variety of *N. odorata* is the soft pink *var. rosea* and its vivid crimson sport 'Rubra'. Both are slightly larger and more vigorous versions of their parent. (1½-2½ ft.) *Var. minor* (1 ft.)

Hybrids Derived from Nymphaea odorata

These hybrids are all derived from *N. odorata* and retain the principal characteristics of that species. Others which may contain some of this species in their make-up, but which do not retain principal characteristics are included with the garden hybrids of unknown or mixed parentage.

EUGENE DE LAND: Exquisite, medium-sized, stellate blooms of deep glowing apricot held high above the water (1½-2 ft.)

EXQUISITA: A small growing variety with rosy-pink stellate flowers. (1 ft.)

FIRECREST: Striking purplish leaves and deep pink flowers with curious red tipped stamens. (1½-3 ft.)

HELEN FOWLER: Enormous heavily scented deep rose flowers which may be up to ten inches across are held above handsome soft green foliage. (1½-3 ft.)

JESSIEANA: Large flowers of a deep shell pink. (1½-2 ft.)

LUCIANA: Fragrant medium sized blooms of a rich deep rose pink that are very similar in shape and form to those of 'Exquisita'. (1½-2 ft.)

SUAVISSIMA: Very fragrant bright rose-pink flowers and luxuriant fresh green foliage. The scent of this variety can be so intense as to be overpowering on a warm still day. (1½-2 ft.)

SULPHUREA: A popular canary yellow variety with dark green heavily mottled foliage. The star-shaped flowers are only slightly fragrant and held clear of the water on short stout stems. A much improved form 'Grandiflora' is larger in every part and is the one usually offered by nurserymen. (1-2 ft.)

TURICENSIS : Medium sized blooms of intense rose-pink. (1½-2½ ft.)

WILLIAM B. SHAW : One of the choicest *odorata* types. Large open creamy-pink heavily scented flowers with deep red internal zoning of the narrowly pointed petals. (1½-2 ft.)

N. tetragona: Pygmy White Waterlily. A tiny white flowering species with small dark green leaves that have distinctive deep purplish undersides. Under favourable conditions fruits are produced in abundance and contain extremely viable seeds which, if sown immediately, will produce flowering size plants within two years. A very variable species with many different geographical forms which exhibit wide differences in leaf size and colouring. The very fine North American *tetragona var. leibergii* with plain green leaves and white flowers with conspicuous purplish lines down the petals is the plant most frequently encountered. (6 in.-1 ft.)

N. tuberosa: Strong growing, almost scentless species, with pure white cup-shaped flowers that will be known to many of the older generation of gardeners as *N. reniformis*. The large green peltate leaves are devoid of the purplish colouring evident in *N. odorata* and are produced from very distinctive long fleshy tubers. There are at least three white cultivars of this species commonly found in cultivation all of which are superior to the type. 'Maxima' and 'Paeslingberg' produce huge ivory goblet-like blooms amidst vigorous soft green foliage, whilst 'Richardsonii' in complete contrast bears superbly rounded blossoms with conspicuous pea-green sepals. A strong growing pink form with sweetly scented blooms, *var. rosea*, is often listed by nurserymen but owing to its exceptionally vigorous growth can only be recommended for large pools or lakes. (2-4 ft.)

Waterlily Hybrids
All the hybrids mentioned below are of unknown or only partially discernible origin. The two very distinctive groups of Laydekeri and Marliacea hybrids and the pygmy varieties are treated as

individual sections, whereas the others are listed in alphabetical order. Consequently, neighbouring varieties of the latter will not necessarily possess the same or even similar botanical characteristics.

ALBATROSS: Medium growing with large pure white blooms which encircle a central boss of golden stamens. Leaves purplish when young but changing to deep green when fully expanded. (1-2 ft.)

AMABILIS: Large pointed salmon-pink flowers which deepen to soft rose with age. The yellow stamens also intensify to a fiery orange. (1½-2½ ft.)

ANDREANA: A vigorous variety with deep crimson blooms that are streaked with white. (2-3 ft.)

ARC-EN-CIEL: An extraordinary hybrid with leaves that are splashed and stained with purple, rose, white and bronze. The flowers which are soft blush are only infrequently produced but nevertheless most attractive. Normally grown for its foliage alone. (1½-2 ft.)

ARETHUSA: Large rounded deep rose-pink flowers intensifying to crimson towards the centre. (1½-2 ft.)

ATTRACTION: The large garnet red flowers of this variety are attractively flecked with white and may be up to nine inches across when fully expanded. (2-4 ft.)

AURORA: A charming little plant with purplish mottled leaves and flowers that change colour day by day. The buds are cream, opening to yellow and finally passing through orange to blood red. (1-1½ ft.)

BARONESS ORCZY: Large deep rose-pink blooms. Excellent for the medium-sized pool. (1½-2 ft.)

BRACKLEYI ROSEA: Sweetly scented rose-pink flowers ageing to flesh pink or white are held clear of the water on short stout stems. Deep green very brittle foliage. Seedlings of varying shades of pink and rose are sometimes offered, but are seldom worth purchasing unless the true variety is unavailable. (2-3 ft.)

CHARLES DE MEURVILLE: An extremely strong growing plant with large plum-coloured blooms that are tipped and streaked with white. Handsome olive green foliage. (2-4 ft.)

COL. A. J. WELCH: A large and rather coarse waterlily with soft canary yellow flowers. Occasionally reproduces viviparously. (2-4 ft.)

COLLOSEA: Possibly the largest and strongest growing pink variety. Dark olive-green leaves crowned with fragrant flesh pink blooms. (2-6 ft.)

COMANCHE: Small deep orange blooms changing to bronze with age. The leaves are purplish when young but rapidly turn green as they unfurl. (1-1½ ft.)

COMTE DE BOUCHARD: Masses of small purplish-red flowers with vivid orange stamens. (1-2 ft.)

CONQUEROR: Large crimson cup-shaped flowers flecked with white. Young foliage purple, eventually changing to green. (1½-2 ft.)

ELLISIANA: Small wine red blooms with orange stamens are produced in abundance. One of the easiest and most reliable waterlilies. I have had plants commence flowering only three weeks after being cut back, divided, and replanted. (1-2 ft.)

ESCARBOUCLE: The most famous and popular red variety. Large crimson flowers up to a foot across with a central boss of golden yellow stamens. A truly magnificent plant. (2-6 ft.)

ESMERALDA: Unusual pink and white variegated stellate flowers. A conversation piece rather than a plant of garden merit. (1½-2 ft.)

EUCHARIS: Soft rose-pink blooms splashed and dappled with white. Very elegant and far superior to the preceding. (1½-2 ft.)

FABIOLA: Warm rosy-red blooms with conspicuous nut brown stamens are borne amidst delicate pale green foliage. (1½-2 ft.)

FROEBELI : Deep blood red flowers with orange stamens and dull purplish-green leaves. One of the most popular and free-flowering varieties for the garden pool. (1½-2 ft.)

GALATEE : White flowers heavily overlaid with red, producing an extraordinary piebald effect. Leaves dark green splashed with maroon. (1½-2 ft.)

GLADSTONIANA : Exceptionally large pure white blooms with bright golden stamens float like huge soup dishes amidst the abundant dark green foliage. (2-8 ft.)

GLOIRE DE TEMPLE SUR LOT : Fragrant fully double flowers of rosy pink incurving petals that change to pure white with age. A shy bloomer for the first two or three years, but well worthwhile establishing. Still very expensive, even young plants of this variety cost several pounds. A plant for the connoisseur. (1½-3 ft.)

GLORIOSA : Very fragrant flowers of deep currant red. Blooms from mid-May until the first frost. Most adaptable and easy going. (1½-3 ft.)

GOLIATH : Large tulip-shaped flowers with unusual creamy-white stamens. The outer petals are white with a rosy blush and shade into apricot petaloides towards the centre. (2-6 ft.)

GONNERE : Double pure white globular flowers with conspicuous green sepals bob amongst luxuriant pea-green leaves. In my opinion this is the finest white variety. (1½-2 ft.)

GRAZIELLA : Orange-red flowers with deep orange stamens, produced in abundance throughout the summer. Olive-green leaves blotched with brown and purple. (1-2 ft.)

HERMINE : Tulip-shaped blooms of the purest white held slightly above the water. Dark-green oval leaves. (1½-2½ ft.)

INDIANA : Orange-red flowers ageing to deep red. Foliage heavily blotched and splashed with purple. (1½-2 ft.)

JAMES BRYDON : Large crimson paeony-shaped flowers which float amidst dark purplish-green leaves that are often flecked with maroon. A great favourite. (1½-3 ft.)

LAYDEKERI HYBRIDS
A group of hybrids suitable for the smaller pool which were raised by the famous hybridiser Marliac and named after his son-in-law Maurice Laydeker. (All 1-2 ft.)

ALBA: Snow-white blooms with yellow stamens which give off a powerful aroma reminiscent of a newly opened packet of tea.

FULGENS: Fragrant bright crimson flowers with reddish stamens. Dark-green leaves with purplish undersides. A slow propagator and always likely to be expensive.

LILACEA: Soft pink fragrant flowers which age to deep rose crimson.

PURPURATA: One of the most outstanding hardy varieties currently available. The rich vinous red flowers are produced from late April until the first autumn frosts. During the height of the flowering season there may be upwards of two dozen blooms on a well established plant at any one time. The leaves are comparatively small, purple beneath, and often marked on the surfaces with black or maroon splashes.

ROSEA: Deep rose cup-shaped flowers. Rather more scarce than its counterparts.

LIVINGSTONE: Small growing, very fragrant variety with slender tulip-shaped blooms of red and white striped petals which surround a central boss of deep mahogany stamens. (1½-2½ ft.)

MARLIACEA HYBRIDS
A group of vigorous hardy varieties suitable for the medium and large pool. Raised by Marliac, these are of indeterminate origin, but include some of the best and easiest varieties a gardener can grow.

ALBIDA: Large pure white fragrant blooms with golden

centres. The sepals and backs of the petals are often flushed with soft pink. Large deep green leaves with red or purplish undersides. (1½-3½ ft.)

CARNEA: (syn. Morning Glory) A very strong flesh-pink hybrid. Flowers on newly established plants are often white for the first few months. An excellent cut flower variety with a strong vanilla fragrance. (1½-5 ft.)

CHROMATELLA: A very old and popular variety. Large soft yellow flowers are produced amidst handsome mottled foliage. (1½-2½ ft.)

FLAMMEA: Fiery red flowers flecked with white are produced amidst striking mottled foliage. Not quite as free-flowering as other hybrids in this group. (1½-2½ ft.)

IGNEA: Deep crimson tulip-shaped blooms above large fresh green leaves. The anthers are bright crimson often merging with their background and producing a quite fascinating effect. (1½-2½ ft.)

ROSEA: Only differs from Marliacea Carnea in the intensity of colouring; its petals being infused with a deep rosy flush. The first coloured waterlily produced by Marliac and well known on this account. (1½-4 ft.)

RUBRA-PUNCTATA: Deep rosy-carmine flowers splashed and spotted with white. (1½-2½ ft.)

MASANIELLO: Fragrant rose-pink, cup-shaped flowers liberally sprinkled with flecks of crimson. Intense orange stamens. (1½-3 ft.)

MAURICE LAYDEKER: One of the smallest varieties. Beautiful vinous red flowers with faint white flecks on the outer petals. A very shy bloomer and slow propagator, but worth growing when *N. Pygmaea Rubra* is not available. (1 ft.)

MOOREI: A very fine soft yellow variety raised in Adelaide Botanic Gardens at the turn of the century. Pale green foliage irregularly sprinkled with purple spots. (1½-2½ ft.)

MRS RICHMOND: Beautiful pale rose-pink flowers that pass to crimson with age. Conspicuous golden stamens. (1½-2½ ft.)

NEWTON: Rosy-peach flowers held high above the water. Bright orange stamens. (1½-2½ ft.)

ODALISQUE: Masses of medium sized soft pink stellate blooms. Light green foliage. I have found this variety to be so prolific as to flower itself to death within two or three years. Must be treated as a temporary inhabitant of the pool and replaced regularly. (1½-2 ft.)

PAUL HARIOT: Very much like a smaller version of 'Moorei' but the blooms intensify to deep orange with age. Handsome purple spotted foliage. (1-1½ ft.)

PHOEBUS: Yellow flowers overlaid with crimson and with centres of intense orange-red stamens. Dark green foliage heavily mottled with purple. (1½-2 ft.)

PRINCESS ELIZABETH: Blooms of delicate cyclamen-pink which intensify with age are held high above the water. Very fragrant. (1½-2½ ft.)

PYGMAEA HYBRIDS
The pygmy varieties are excellent subjects for sinks, troughs or pools where the water does not exceed a foot in depth, or on the marginal shelves of larger pools.

ALBA: The tiniest white waterlily. Each bloom measures no more than an inch across and is a complete replica of its larger cousins. Small oval, dark-green leaves with purple reverses.

HELVOLA: Beautiful canary yellow flowers with orange stamens produced continuously throughout the summer. Olive-green foliage heavily mottled with purple and brown.

JOHANN PRING: Deep pink flowers up to two inches across with a central boss of orange stamens.

RUBRA: Tiny blood red flowers with orange stamens float

amidst purplish-green leaves. Slow to propagate and consequently very expensive.

ROSE AREY: The best of the rose-pink varieties. Large open stellate flowers with a central boss of golden stamens and an overpowering aniseed fragrance. Fine plain green leaves. (1½-2½ ft.)

ROSE NYMPH: An exceptionally fine pink variety with large fragrant flowers some six inches across. A connoisseur's plant that requires careful cultivation if one is to do it justice. (1-1½ ft.)

SEIGNOURETTII: Bright orange-red flowers with a buff reverse. Foliage green spotted with chestnut. (1½-2½ ft.)

SIOUX: Almost identical to 'Aurora'. Pale yellow blooms passing through orange to crimson. Purplish mottled foliage. (1-1½ ft.)

SOLFATARE: Soft yellow stellate blooms with a rosy-red flush. Dark-green mottled foliage. (1-2 ft.)

SOMPTUOSA: An early flowering waterlily with large fragrant double pink blooms. The stamens are orange and contrast markedly with the soft velvety petals. (1-2 ft.)

SUNRISE: An outstanding variety of American origin. Large fragrant soft canary-yellow flowers up to eight inches across and dull green leaves occasionally blotched with brown, and with reddish undersides. Plants of this variety make a marvellous show in a pool at the Royal Horticultural Society's gardens at Wisley. Owing to the excessive demand for this variety, and the consequently high prices received by growers, gardeners should be wary of purchasing plants without first of all checking their identity. This can be done by inspecting the undersides of the leaves and the leaf stalks for fine bristly hairs. If these are present then the plants are almost certainly 'Sunrise'. (1½-3½ ft.)

VESUVE: Large amaranth-red flowers flecked and shaded with orange. Reddish-green leaves. (1-1½ ft.)

VIRGINALIS: A real gem for the medium sized pool. Wonderful semi-double flowers of the purest white float amidst pea-green lily pads. Slow to become established but well worth waiting for. Always likely to be expensive as it is very reluctant to produce suitable propagating material. ($1\frac{1}{2}$-$2\frac{1}{2}$ ft.)

WILLIAM FALCONER : Medium sized upright blood-red flowers with yellow stamens. Foliage purplish when young but changing to deep olive-green with age. ($1\frac{1}{2}$-$2\frac{1}{2}$ ft.)

OTHER DEEP WATER AQUATICS

Apart from the Nymphaeas there are several other aquatic plants which will grow happily in the deeper areas of the pool. Although not as spectacular as the waterlilies they do merit consideration for inclusion in all but the tiniest of pools.

APONOGETON Water Hawthorn

The Aponogetons are exotic-looking and generally tender aquatics which are probably more familiar to aquarists than pond-keepers. However, the South African *Aponogeton distachyus* is absolutely hardy and a very reliable pond plant. Not only does it remain almost evergreen, but will also provide a continuous display of bloom from April until November, or even Christmas during mild winters. The individual flowers are forked into two arms and bear a double row of bract-like organs at the base of which are clusters of jet-black stamens. This gives a most striking effect and coupled with its powerful vanilla fragrance makes it a most desirable acquisition. Up to two dozen flowering stems may be borne on a plant at any one time and these float on the water amidst dull green, more or less oblong leaves, that are often heavily splashed and spotted with purple.

Several old gardening and botanical books recognise the existence of red or pink forms of the species, such as *A. distachyus* 'Rubra' and *A.d.* 'Rosea'. But I have not come across any of these and am inclined to believe that the reddish colour was caused by environmental conditions. I have noted that after a frost, open flowers will turn pink and remain that colour for several days. Plants growing in shallow water, between two and six inches deep, often produce a reddish colouring, but on being transferred to the deeper water of an aquarium revert to the original white.

Apart from *A. distachyus*, there is another African species, *A. krauseanus*, which is occasionally encountered and certainly well worth acquiring should the opportunity arise. Its blooms are almost identical to those of its cousin, being forked and heavily scented but are completely white and devoid of the black stamens. Unfortunately it is not reliably hardy, except in the southern-most counties, and is best removed to a tub or tank in the greenhouse for the winter months. Both species like a depth in excess of eighteen inches, where they will seed freely and form splendid colonies of fine young plants.

BRASENIA   Water Shield
Until recent years the common Water Shield or Water Target, *Brasenia schreberi*, (syn. *B. peltata*), was regarded as a similar proposition to *Aponogeton krauseanus*, but it has been known to come through recent hard winters unscathed. Closely related to the Nymphaeas, this plant thrives in acid water between one and three feet deep, where its slender creeping rootstock can colonise an open sunny position unimpeded. It is not as pernicious as many other water plants and can be rapidly outgrown by waterlilies and even the modest water hawthorn if not carefully watched. The fleshy rounded leaves are about two inches across and supported by long central leaf stalks that are arranged alternately along the slender brittle stem.

From the axils, bright purple three or four petalled floating flowers are produced, followed by curious seed pods each containing one or two seeds that are dispersed when a lid on top of the fruit breaks free. If collected and sown immediately in trays of wet mud, these provide a ready means of propagation.

NUPHAR   Spatterdock
These are usually regarded as poor relations of the Nymphaea, but what they lack in the way of flowers they more than compensate for with their ease of cultivation and adaptability to situation. They will thrive in dense shade or full sun, fast streams or stagnant ponds and there are varieties to suit all depths from a few inches up to eight feet. Most varieties have beautiful membraneous translucent submerged foliage and some of the smaller kinds are often

used by aquarists as centre-pieces in cold-water aquaria. Cultivation is identical to that afforded the various Nymphaea species and propagation by division, although eyes are sometimes produced.

The Spatterdock Species and Their Varieties
N. advenum: American Spatterdock, Moose-root. A popular and fairly common variety that will grow in almost any position. Some of the large thick fresh green leaves float on the surface, whilst others stand erect from the central crown. The globular yellow flowers are about three inches across, tinged with purple or green, and have bright coppery-red stamens. A very variable species which has recently been overhauled taxonomically so that it is now subdivided into further varieties, species and sub-species based principally on leaf shape. A cream and green variegated form *var. variegatum (syn. americanum)* is sometimes encountered. This has soft yellow flowers and produces only floating foliage, never the stiff, erect kind. (1½-5 ft.)

N. japonicum: This is a very fine yellow flowered species from Japan which needs growing in still water if it is to give of its best. The large floating leaves are slender and more or less arrow-shaped, whilst the submerged ones are curly and of a delicate membraneous nature. A very popular variety, *var. rubrotinctum* has glowing orange flowers with striking red-tipped stamens, whilst *var. variegatum* has cream and green mottled foliage that is entirely erect. (1-3½ ft.)

N. juranum: A rare and diminutive species from eastern France with tiny yellow flowers. Once believed lost to cultivation, but now making a come back. (1-1½ ft.)

N. lutea: Yellow Pond Lily, Brandy Bottle. Bottle-shaped yellow flowers which emit a slightly offensive alcoholic odour are produced amidst masses of leathery ovate floating leaves. A vigorous growing native which should be used only sparingly. Its various forms are only a trifle more endearing, *var. sericeum* with its large intense yellow flowers and *var. sericeum denticulatum* with slightly dentate foliage are probably the two nicest. *Nuphar lutea var. rubropetalum* has similar blooms with an infusion of red, while those of *var. purpureosignatum* have curious purplish markings (1-6 ft.)

N. macrophyllum: Large oval glabrous leaves and tiny rounded flowers of an intense canary-yellow are produced from a predominantly green knobbly rootstock. (1-5 ft.)

N. microphyllum: (syn. *N. kalmianum*). A delightful little fellow with crispy membraneous underwater foliage and quaint pea-green floating leaves. Its bright yellow flowers are less than an inch across but borne in profusion throughout the summer. (1-1½ ft.)

N. orbiculatum: A vigorous plant with bright green pubescent leaves and pale yellow blooms about two inches in diameter. A native of the southern states of America, this species may not always prove to be hardy in the colder areas of the country. (1-5 ft.)

N. polysepalum: An excellent plant for shallower water where it will rapidly become covered in golden blossoms up to six inches across. These look like precious golden goblets amid the deep green sea of lanceolate floating foliage. (1-3 ft.)

N. pumila: (syn. N. minimum). Dwarf Pond Lily. Least Yellow Pond Lily. A splendid little plant for the shallows of a pool, or in a sink or rock pool. The tiny pale yellow blooms are produced amidst small heart-shaped leaves with deeply cut basal sinus. The variety *N. pumila var. affine* has even smaller flowers and pale lime-green leaves. (1-1½ ft.)

N. rubrodiscum: Red Disced Pond Lily. Large yellow flowers with bright crimson central stigmatic discs and handsome dark green foliage. The underwater leaves are crinkled whilst the floating ones are long, spear-shaped and occasionally erect. (1-3 ft.)

N. sagittifolium: Cape Fear Spatterdock. Soft yellow flowers nestle amidst broad glossy floating leaves and are followed by curious dull green marble-like fruits. More usually grown in a cold-water aquarium than outside, but well worth trying in milder districts. (1-1½ ft.)

SPATTERDOCK HYBRIDS

JAPONICUM × PUMILA: A recent and as yet unnamed hybrid which is receiving wide acclaim, particularly from cold-water aquarium fanciers. However, it appears to be hardy and produces the yellow flowers of *N. japonicum* whilst retaining the broad translucent underwater foliage of *N. pumila*. (1-1½ ft.)

SPENNERANA: (*N. lutea var. minor; N. intermedia*). Hybrid Yellow Pond Lily. A natural hybrid thought to be between *N. lutea* and *N. pumila*. Small yellow flowers with prominent star-like ovaries amongst clusters of broad light green leaves. (1-2 ft.)

NYMPHOIDES Water Fringe

A splendid group of plants formerly known as Villarsia or Limnan-themum, of which only one species is reliably hardy. This is the native water fringe, *Nymphoides peltata (syn. Villarsia nym-phoides)*. During late summer it provides a wonderful display of delicate yellow fringed buttercup-like flowers amidst handsome green and brown mottled foliage reminiscent of a pygmy waterlily. For this reason it has often been dubbed 'the poor man's waterlily' and certainly is useful where there are large expanses of water to be clothed and inadequate finances to stock with Nymphaeas. A variety listed as '*Bennettii*' looks almost identical to me, but has foliage almost entirely devoid of brownish markings. All varieties of Nymphoides can be grown from seed, but more usually from division of the travelling rootstocks. (9 ins-2½ ft.)

ORONTIUM Golden Club

The golden club (*Orontium aquaticum*), is one of the most bizarre and adaptable plants one can introduce into the garden pool. Grow-ing either in wet mud or eighteen inches of water—but preferring the latter—this curious member of the Arum family makes a striking display during April and early May with golden-yellow pencil-like flowers which stand out of the water above waxy glaucous floating foliage. Small greenish fruits often follow and, if allowed to ripen and the seed sown in pans of wet soil, form a ready means of propagation.

MARGINAL PLANTS

As intimated earlier, marginal plants are those that grow in the shallows around the edges of natural ponds. In the garden pool, however, they are accommodated on specially constructed shelves, either planted directly into soil spread along their length or else in baskets in the same manner as prescribed for waterlilies. The growing medium should also be basically of a similar nature; any necessary additions or special requirements for particular species being located under the respective generic heading.

For the purposes of this book, marginal plants are going to be taken as those that require between one and nine inches of water to give of their best, although it should be appreciated that some will grow quite satisfactorily in wet soil, or in some cases, water that is in excess of nine inches.

ACORUS Sweet Flag

Although members of the Arum family, the various species of Acorus are often taken to be Irises on account of their clumps of flat linear leaves and fat fleshy rhizomes. The Common Sweet Flag, *Acorus calamus*, is undoubtedly the most familiar with shiny fresh green foliage and curious greenish yellow horn-like flower spikes. Although not strictly a native, this plant has been naturalised in Britain for over three hundred years and become well established in many localities. Indeed, its leaves were formerly woven into mats so that when trodden on the faint aroma of tangerines which they emitted would be wafted through the air. However, from a strictly horticultural point of view it is completely outshone by the vastly superior, but much slower growing, cream, green and rose variegated form *A.c.* 'Variegatus'.

A diminutive grassy leafed Japanese species *A. gramineus* and its variegated form are sometimes offered by nurserymen and are excellent for shallow water in tiny ponds. There appears to be very little difference between these and the aquarium plants grown by aquarists as *A. pusillus* and *A. pusillus* 'Variegatus' and some authorities consider one to be a mere variant of the other, so it can be assumed that when purchasing a plant, no matter which version of the name is used, a diminutive hardy subject of great merit will be acquired.

ALISMA   Water Plantain

On account of their pernicious seeding habits the various species of Alisma are often despised or at least distrusted by experienced pond-owners. However, there are four very interesting species that can be relied upon to behave themselves reasonably well. Of these the most familiar is *Alisma plantago-aquatica*, a handsome native with attractive ovate foliage and loose pyramidal panicles of pink and white flowers. The broad towering spires become hard and woody after flowering and persist throughout the winter, catching the snow on their outspread arms, in a most attractive manner.

The North American *A. parviflora* is of similar habit, but with distinct rounded leaves that during autumn and winter fall into the water and become completely and most beautifully skeletonised. Its pyramids of pink and white flowers are shorter than those of its illustrious cousin and render it more suitable for the smaller pool.

Both the Floating Water Plantain, *A. natans* and the diminutive *A. ranunculoides* (now more correctly known as *Baldellia ranunculoides*) are of similar disposition and can easily be accommodated in a tub or sink. The former is a very interesting and singularly attractive species with tiny floating foliage and solitary snow white blossoms each with a distinctive yellow blotch. It requires to be permanently immersed, disliking intensely the wet muddy conditions its contemporaries enjoy. Indeed *A. ranunculoides* is best cultivated under such conditions, its delicate arching stems bending down and rooting wherever they touch the moist medium, forming a dense spreading colony of bright green lanceolate foliage studded throughout late summer and early autumn with crowded umbels of rose and blush flowers.

ANEMOPSIS   Apache Beads

An uncommon aquatic of American origin closely allied to the popular Houttuynia. Although not always considered as absolutely hardy, this unusual perennial is well worthwhile acquiring should the opportunity arise. The genus as far as I am aware is restricted to one species, *Anemopsis californica*, a somewhat ungainly plant of anemone-like appearance with flowers that consist of a hard cone or 'spadix' surrounded by a single whorl of pearly white petal-like bracts. Only in damp mud or shallow water with an alkaline tendency is this little fellow really at home, but then he will grow with great gusto forming sizeable clumps that can be readily divided. The roots have an overpowering fragrance of a somewhat sickly nature and were used for medicinal purposes in former years.

BUTOMUS   Flowering Rush
Butomus umbellatus is the only species and a widely distributed native of Europe and temperate Asia. Throughout August and September this handsome aquatic produces spreading umbels of dainty rose-pink flowers on stout erect flower stems which ascend through masses of narrow triquetrous foliage. Propagation is easily affected by collecting the small bulbils which appear in the axils of the leaves and pushing them into mud under two or three inches of water.

CALLA   Bog Arum
Calla palustris is a splendid plant for masking the edge of the pool, spreading in all directions by means of stout creeping rhizomes clothed in handsome glossy heart-shaped leaves. Its flowers belie the plant's close affinity to Zantedeschia—the florists' Arum—being smaller, but otherwise almost identical, and borne like tiny white sails in a sea of dark-green foliage. They are succeeded by spikes of succulent red berries filled with viable seed which, if sown immediately it ripens, forms a quick and inexpensive means of propagation. The winter buds that form on the long trailing rhizomes can also be removed, and if placed in trays of wet mud soon take root and form healthy young plants.

CALTHA   Marsh Marigold or Kingcup
There can be few people who are not familiar with our native Marsh Marigold, *Caltha palustris*, an outstanding swamp plant with dark-green foliage that is garlanded during late spring with waxy blooms of an intense golden-yellow. A number of variants are recognised by botanists of which *Caltha palstris ssp. palustris* and

C. palustris ssp. minor are the most commonly encountered and occasionally listed by nurserymen.

However, from a horticultural point of view only the mutant *C. palustris ssp. minor plena* with small double button-like flowers and the cultivar form *C. palustris* 'Flore Pleno' are worth seeking. The latter in particular is a plant of outstanding merit bearing a profusion of waxy fully double flowers of the deepest golden yellow. Although commercially exploited, stocks of this plant are never plentiful and prices often high for this class of plant, but I can unreservedly guarantee that the purchaser will get more than an ample return for his investment. Not so with its white flowered cousin, *C. palustris alba*, a greatly over-rated plant with small single off-white flowers with golden yellow stamens and dull, rounded, scalloped leaves. The power of the pen has brought this plant to the fore in the last decade, its praises being sung by journalists who can never have seen its paltry flowers or mildew ridden foliage.

The much neglected Mountain Marigold, *C. leptosepala*, is a far better proposition, producing broad white blooms with a distinctive silvery tinge above splendid dark-green foliage. A variety of this, *C. leptosepala grandiflora*, has even larger white flowers and foliage of corresponding magnitude. But this is not the giant of the family for this title must surely rest with the Himalayan Marsh Marigold, *C. polypetala*, which has dark-green leaves quite ten inches across and huge trusses of golden yellow flowers on stems some three feet high.

However, all the species no matter what size, shape, or colour are extremely tolerant of situation, growing equally well in wet soil or a foot of water, but being more compact and attractive under drier conditions. Propagation of the double forms is by division as they are incapable of setting seed and is also more convenient for the natural species as germination can be erratic and the resultant plants extremely variable.

CAREX Sedges
An extensive family of Sedges mostly of little garden value and with an unfortunate tendency to become invasive if not selected

with great care. The often recommended Cyperus Sedge, *C. pseudo-cyperus*, is one such species, a glabrous tufted perennial with a rapidly spreading rootstock. It somewhat resembles a coarse Umbrella Grass—*Cyperus alternifolius* of the florist—but with sparse dark-green foliage and curious spiked inflorescences that droop from their slender supports.

An even more evasive native best avoided is the Great Pond Sedge, *C. riparia*, but a few words in praise of its cultivar forms should not come amiss. These are very restrained and give an almost oriental charm to the water garden. Probably the most well known is *C. riparia* 'Bowles Golden', a much prized plant with rich golden foliage and spikes of dark brown flowers. I find it most temperamental until established in a situation to its liking and even then it tends to die out if subjected to persistent flooding during winter.

A plant known as *C. riparia* 'Aurea' is sometimes offered by nurserymen, but I have yet to discover the difference between this and 'Bowles Golden'. *C. riparia* 'Variegata', however, is quite distinct for the leaves are attractively striped with white and green. This is an easier and far more reliable plant which thrives in partial shade in anything up to three or four inches of water. Care should be taken not to confuse it with the very similar, *C. morrowii* 'Variegata', for although most striking, this cannot be recommended as a permanent pool-side resident in any but the mildest of areas, and if grown at all should be confined to the cool greenhouse.

Few other species can be said to be worthy of consideration, with the exception of our native pendulous sedge, *C. pendula*, and only this where space is not at a premium. It is a tall dignified plant with broad green leaves and long drooping spikes of khaki catkin-like flowers that is commonly encountered along shady streamsides and in damp woods in many parts of the British Isles. Propagation of natural species is by seed, whilst those with variegated or golden foliage respond reasonably well to careful division.

COTULA Brass Buttons
Although the majority of members of this large family of Composite plants are terrestrial and indeed often useful rock garden subjects, at least one, *C. coronopifolia*, is truly aquatic and being

small, of immense value around the margins of tiny rock garden and patio pools. Its bright golden flowers are like a smaller version of those of a Dandelion and borne in profusion above strongly scented light green foliage. Unfortunately it is a monocarpic species, dying as soon as flowering is over, but if left undisturbed usually seeds itself and is then all but in name a perennial.

CYPERUS Umbrella Grass
Only two species of this predominantly tropical genus are sufficiently hardy to withstand the vagaries of our winter climate and experts are even divided as to the hardiness of one of these, *C. vegetus (syn. C. eragrostis)*. However, in the light of my own personal experience I would say that it is absolutely hardy and well worth planting in the shallow margins of large and medium sized pools. A native of Chile, it produces tufted spikelets of reddish mahogany flowers throughout late summer from amidst spreading umbels of bright pea-green foliage.

Its larger cousin the Sweet Galingale, *C. longus*, is a similar kind of plant. A trifle taller, and with terminal umbels of stiff spiky leaves which radiate from the stem like the ribs of an umbrella, this stout fellow is never more happy than when growing on a bank and allowed to creep down and colonise the mud at the water's edge. Both grow readily from seed or division of the creeping rootstocks.

DAMASONIUM Starfruit or Thrumwort
Damasonium alisma (syn. D. stellatum) is a very rare native of relatively little horticultural merit, but one of which I am very fond. Its flower spikes are stout and upright with whorls of milky-white blooms followed by curious star shaped fruits full of viable seed. The leaves are strap shaped and arise from a hard corm-like rootstock which in large plants will divide for propagation purposes.

DECODON Water Willow or Swamp Loosestrife
Coarse perennials of little value to the small pool-owner, but very useful in large expanses of water where they can be allowed to become naturalised. *Decodon verticillatus (syn. Nesaea verticillata)*, an American native with tall willowy stems and sprays of rose pink

tubular flowers, is most commendable on account of its delightful autumnal tints. Pinkish at the approach of autumn, by the first hard winter frosts arrive to defoliage it, the leaves have passed through rose and vermilion to an intense fiery crimson. Propagation is by cuttings, division, or detaching fallen stems that often root along their entire length when in contact with water or mud.

ERIOPHORUM   Cotton Grass
The cotton grasses are extremely useful subjects for shallow margins, particularly in ponds with a tendency towards acidity. There are twenty-one known species with a distribution which ranges from the arctic and northern temperate regions to South Africa. All are absolutely hardy but unfortunately few seem to be in general cultivation. Our native *Eriophorum angustifolium (syn. E. polystachyon)* is the one commonly commercialised and undoubtedly the most useful. With its evergreen grassy foliage and cotton wool-like seeding heads it makes a welcome contribution to the pool side during May and early June.

A similar, but larger species, the broad-leafed cotton grass, *E. latifolium*, is sometimes encountered but seems to be very short-lived under cultivation. However, anyone who can successfully establish a clump will be well rewarded with a memorable display of dainty pendant spikelets of cotton wool, which if picked in their full glory, dry admirably for floral decoration. Both species are readily propagated by division.

GLYCERIA   Manna Grass
Of the many aquatic species of Glyceria only one selection of our native *Glyceria aquatica (syn. G. spectabilis)* can be recommended for the water garden. This is *G.a. variegata*, a handsome perennial grass with cream and green striped foliage which on emerging in early spring are infused with a deep rosy-pink. Propagation has to be by division, seed being of poor germination and giving rise to all manner of bastard forms.

GRATIOLA   Hedge Hyssop
A family of some twenty or so species of annual and perennial herbs of dubious garden merit, but of great interest on account of

their alleged medicinal properties. A decoction of the roots and leaves of *Gratiola officinalis* and several other lesser known species is said to be of great benefit in treating bruises. The not infrequently encountered *G. officinalis* is a delicate plant with pretty serrated foliage and small blue flowers. Propagation by seed.

HIPPURIS   Mare's Tail
The Common Mare's Tail, *Hippuris vulgaris*, is an often despised plant, particularly in places where it grows locally abundantly and makes itself a nuisance. For this reason it is seldom recommended for the garden pool and possibly rightly so, but in a shady pond or fast moving stream it is the ideal plant, thriving in adversity and thrusting up simple but not unattractive spikes of narrow whorled leaves. Propagation by division.

HOUTTUYNIA
This is a monotypic genus, the lone species, *H. cordata (syn. H. foetida)*, being a most amenable subject for the small and medium sized pool. It has handsome bluish-green heart-shaped leaves and white four petalled flowers with hard central cones, although in the double form 'Plena' these are lost in a dense central ruff of petals. An excellent marginal plant that should be allowed to creep about at will and carpet the ground beneath taller growing rushes. Propagation by division.

HYPERICUM   St. John's Wort
The Marsh Hypericum, *Hypericum elodes*, is an extremely useful native plant for shallow water or wet mud. Forming a dense carpet of foliage it hides the often ugly point where pool meets land and gives an added bonus of showy yellow flowers during late summer. Propagation by division or cuttings rooted in a pot or tray of mud.

IRIS
Until recent years much confusion existed amongst growers of irises as to which forms and species were actually aquatic. This was generated, doubtless unwittingly, by the Japanese who collected irises from the wild and sent them over to this country in large numbers. These were all either *Iris kaempferi*, *I. laevigata* or hybrids between the two and all to the inexperienced looked identical.

However, when planted in water only the *I. laevigata* would survive the winter, which gave rise to a lot of uneasiness amongst early growers of these plants as to their usefulness. Fortunately, some wide-eyed botanist discovered the existence of the two species—which can easily be separated by the presence of a prominent midrib in the leaves of *I. kaempferi* and its absence in those of *I. laevigata*—and the mystery was solved.

Iris kaempferi is now considered to be more of a marsh plant as it will not tolerate being submerged during the winter months, whereas, *I. laevigata* is entirely aquatic, living permanently with its feet in water. The latter is the very popular blue iris of the Asian paddy fields and produces typical sky blue flowers during June. Many cultivars are commonly available and even if of slightly dubious origin enjoy much the same conditions as *I. laevigata*. *Iris laevigata* 'Alba' which is white, 'Monstrosa' (*syn.* 'Colchesteri') violet and white, and 'Rose Queen' are the most outstanding, together with the handsome cream and green variegated foliage form with soft blue flowers which is known variously as 'Elegantissima' and 'Variegata'.

Everyone is undoubtedly familiar with our native Yellow Flag, *Iris pseudacorus*, a stout prolific grower with broad sword-like leaves and attractive reddish seed capsules. But it is rather too coarse for the smaller pool and better replaced by one of its varieties *var. bastardi* soft primrose blooms, 'Golden Queen' refined golden yellow or 'Variegata' with golden and green striped foliage.

The North American counterpart of our Yellow Flag is *Iris versicolor*, a splendid fellow with violet blue flowers veined with purple and with a conspicuous patch of yellow on the falls. Its variety 'Kermesina' is even more lovely, the blooms being of a gorgeous deep plum shade with the same distinctive markings. All the natural species of iris grow readily from seed or can be divided as is obviously essential with the named garden forms.

JUNCUS Rushes
The True Rushes or Juncus species are not normally considered desirable for the garden pool for, with few exceptions, they quickly become weedy and rampant, swamping their more sophisticated

neighbours. However, those that are tolerable are some of the most interesting and curious aquatics a keen pool-owner can acquire. Two of the best and most readily obtainable are mutants of our native Soft Rush, *Juncus effusus*, a common inhabitant of wet pastures and marshes throughout the northern hemisphere. The corkscrew rush, *Juncus effuses* 'Spiralis', is a form with curiously malformed stems that grow in a spiralling corkscrew fashion giving the plant a strangely grotesque appearance like a Harry Lauder Walking Stick, while *J. effuses* 'Vittatus' (*syn. J.e.* 'Aureo-striatus') is a golden variegated cultivar which grows about two feet high with alternate longitudinal stripes of green and yellow. As with many variegated plants, normal vigorous green foliage will often swamp the variegated, so destruction of any predominantly green shoots that emerge is essential. Propagation of the cultivar forms is by division.

LUDWIGIA   False Loosestrife
Although most species of Ludwigia are considered as aquarium plants, one local native *L. palustris*, is particularly useful in natural ponds. Although its flowers are petalless and insignificant its foliage is very fine and possesses excellent oxygenating properties. Propagation is by cuttings or division.

MENTHA   Mint
The strongly aromatic Water Mint, *Mentha aquatica*, enjoys shallow water or wet mud at the poolside and when growing happily produces throughout late summer dense terminal whorls of lilac pink flowers on slender reddish stems amidst an abundance of hairy greyish-green foliage. Unfortunately, it is inclined to spread rather rapidly by means of its slender white rhizomes and therefore cannot be recommended for the smaller pool. Many hybrids exist between this and other species, and coupled with the fact that female plants will often produce smaller flowers than the type, one cannot always be sure of having the true plant. But from a horticultural point of view this would seem of little account as all seem to be equally free flowering and prolific. Propagation is by division of the creeping rhizome.

MENYANTHES   Bog Bean or Buck Bean

The Bog Bean, *Menyanthes trifoliata*, is another most distinctive plant for shallow water. It bears decorative white fringed flowers during May above dark green trifoliate leaves, not unlike those of a broad bean. Both the leaves and flowers are protected by a short scaly sheath situated towards the end of each sprawling olive green rhizome and the latter, if chopped into sections each with a root attached, form a successful means of propagation.

MIMULUS   Musk

Most of the members of this very showy family appreciate damp conditions, but only one could strictly speaking be called a permanent perennial aquatic. This is the dainty blue flowered eastern North American *M. ringens*, a delicate looking plant with much branched slender stems and handsome narrow leaflets. It normally grows about eighteen inches high and although it seldom seeds itself, can be readily propagated by stem cuttings about two inches long inserted in pots of wet mud.

Whilst discussing the various Mimulus it would only be fair to mention our native *M. luteus* and its various cultivar forms. Although seldom permanent residents of the pool, they do occasionally seed and naturalise themselves amongst other marginals, or with the gardener's help they can be perpetuated by cuttings over-wintered in a cold frame. They are certainly worth considering where a blaze of colour and informality are the keynotes to the pool's appeal. *Mimulus luteus* as its name implies is yellow; but it is a striking yellow, comparable with that of a sunflower or buttercup and in dense spikes of antirrhinum-like flowers.

Variations and contrasts in colour are provided by hybrids such as the vivid red 'Bonfire', pastel coloured 'Monarch Strain' and the boldly spotted 'Queen's Prize' and 'Tigrinus' strains. For rock pools or the sink garden there is the diminutive 'Whitecroft Scarlet', a little dear of dubious origin but with bright green carpeting foliage and brilliant scarlet hooded flowers, whilst those with a taste for the unusual would probably appreciate the almost double 'Hose-in-Hose' with yellow blooms that consist of one flower inside the other.

MYOSOTIS Forget-me-not

Everyone is familiar with the popular bedding forget-me-not so
frequently seen in parks and gardens during spring, but few are
aware of its delightful cousin the Water Forget-me-not, *M. palustris*,
or as the purists would now have it, *M. scorpioides*. During early
summer this charming little native is absolutely smothered in sky
blue flowers that resemble almost exactly those of its terrestrial
counterpart. An improved variety known as 'Semperflorens' is
decidedly superior to the type, producing fewer leaves and being
less inclined to straggle across the mud. Some years ago a cultivar
called 'Mermaid' was introduced and is often still listed, but as far
as I can tell is no different from the typical species.

Seed raising is the most usual means of propagation, although
division of emerging young crowns early in the spring is normally
successful. The former method, however, has the added advantage
that a plant or two of the white form may be raised. Although not
quite as robust, it makes an unusual and extremely attractive addition when planted amongst the azure hummocks of its conventional
neighbours.

NARTHECIUM Bog Asphodel

Although there are several species of Narthecium suitable for the
water garden, only our native *N. ossifragum* appears to be in cultivation. This is a diminutive plant with a wiry creeping rootstock
and small fans of reddish-green iris-like foliage amidst which are
produced terminal racemes of bright yellow flowers. Although a
useful plant for the bog or sink garden, it cannot be unreservedly
recommended for the margins of the pool as it does not seem to
tolerate any permanent significant depth of water over the crown.
Propagation by seed or division.

NASTURTIUM Water Cress

The Water Cress, known variously as *Nasturtium officinale* and
Rorippa nasturtium-aquaticum, is loved and cherished by all, but
should strictly speaking not be contained within the pages of this
book. Its inclusion, however, follows several years of experience
of dealing with pool-owning customers on our family nursery,
which indicates that any book which attempts to instruct com-

prehensively on the cultivation of aquatic plants must make a special mention of the requirements of this subject if it is to be at all complete.

Generally speaking it can be assumed that in the confines of the average garden pool the successful cultivation of water cress is well nigh impossible, particularly if one wishes to grow choice subjects such as Nymphaeas as well, for water cress requires running water if it is to proliferate—conditions which Nymphaeas and other desirable aquatics in general abhor. However, appreciating the challenge which such a plant offers and the renowned unbending persistence of the average British gardener, it is almost certain that many pool-owners will attempt the feat. In which case I would recommend they try the white and green variegated *N. officinale variegatum*, an unusual plant of exceeding beauty. Propagation is by cuttings which root quite readily in mud beneath a couple of inches of water.

PELTANDRA   Arrow Arum
Two species of this unusual family of arum-like aquatics are sometimes encountered in cultivation. The handsome *Peltandra virginica* has narrow spathes of a pea-green colour borne amidst dark green glossy arrow-shaped foliage which arise from a short fleshy rootstock that readily divides to form new plants, whilst *P. alba (syn. P. saggittaefolia)* has slightly larger greenish or white spathes but is otherwise almost identical. Although *P. alba* is a larger and marginally superior garden plant, it does not appear to be generally available in this country, whereas I know of at least two nurserymen who hold stocks of *P. virginica*.

PHRAGMITES   Spire Reed or Water Bamboo
The strong growing native *Phragmites communis (syn. Arundo phragmites)* is a vigorous bamboo-like perennial that will grow in almost any soil or situation. In the garden pool it should be severely restricted by being planted in a small basket or pot. This usually restrains its enthusiasm for travel, yet does not prevent it thrusting up its handsome silvery-white or purplish silky flower heads. However, to be really effective it requires ample space and needs planting in drifts around a large pool or lake, for here it is more in con-

formity with its surroundings. Apart from the typical species there is a small variegated form *P. communis var. variegatus* which is an outstanding plant worthy of cultivation in all but the tiniest of pools. Propagation is by severing the runners, each with a shoot, and planting where they are required.

POLYGONUM   Willow Grass or Amphibious Bistort
The native *Polygonum amphibium* familiar in many natural ponds and slow-moving streams is not infrequently recommended for the garden pool. Providing it is strictly controlled it can be useful, flowering during late summer with dense rose-red terminal spikes held just above its green or purplish floating foliage, it provides colour at a time when most marginals are beginning to look weary. Propagation by division.

PONTEDERIA   Pickerel Weed
The North American Pickerel Weed, *Pontederia cordata*, is a plant of noble proportions, producing numerous stems each consisting of an ovate or lanceolate shiny green leaf and a leafy bract from which the spike of soft blue flowers emerges. It attains a height of some two or three feet and flowers during August and September. Propagation is usually by division of the rootstocks in early spring or from seed sown whilst still green, although with the latter method results are extremely erratic.

PRESLIA
Preslia cervina is a very desirable aquatic which one not infrequently encounters and, indeed, one which in recent years has grown in popularity. It forms spreading clumps of slender erect stems densely clothed in small lanceolate leaves, and is crowned during late summer with stiff whorled spikes of dainty ultramarine or lilac flowers. The whole plant is strongly aromatic and is happiest when growing in very shallow water. Propagation is by short stem cuttings taken during spring and inserted in pots of wet mud.

RANUNCULUS   Spearwort
The genus Ranunculus is one of massive proportions embracing all the species of buttercup, numerous submerged oxygenating

plants—the Crowfoots—and several interesting marsh plants known collectively as the Spearworts.

Our native *Ranunculus lingua*, the Greater Spearwort, is the largest species and has erect hollow stems well clothed with narrow dark-green leaves and produces large golden flowers in abundance throughout the summer. A natural octaploid variant, *R. lingua* 'Grandiflora', is the plant commonly grown and is an even larger and finer subject.

For those with a limited amount of space the diminutive *R. flammula* or Lesser Spearwort is more appropriate. Like a superior buttercup, it bears glistening golden blooms above dark-green oval leaves and slender reddish stems which in the varieties *R. flammula* var. *tenuifolius* and *R. flammula ssp. scoticus*, scramble across the mud, rooting at every node. Propagation is by separating the emerging shoots during early spring and planting them separately.

RUMEX Dock

The Water Dock, *Rumex hydrolapathum*, is a handsome plant attaining a height of six or eight feet under favourable conditions. Only suitable for the really large pond, it is an enlarged version of the common Garden Dock, but with bold dark-green foliage that changes colour through bronze to crimson in the autumn. A variety *R. hydrolapathum var. maximus*, from Manchuria, is of slightly smaller stature but with larger leaves and is really the most attractive of the two. Both propagate readily from seed or by division of the long woody roots.

SAGITTARIA Arrowhead or Duck Potato

The Arrowheads are marginal plants of a happy disposition, growing equally well in wet mud or a couple of feet of water. They spread quite quickly by means of runners, which at the approach of winter develop large ovoid turions or winter buds at their extremities. These look like iris bulbs and are popularly known as duck potatoes as wild ducks will forage about in the mud and dig them up during the winter months if given the opportunity.

Sagittaria saggittifolia and *S. japonica* are the most popular species, although many botanists and horticulturists lump the two together and refer to them as *S. sagittifolia*. However, to

Caltha palustris, the common Marsh Marigold or Kingcup.

Caltha polypetala, the Himalayan Marsh Marigold. This has dark green leaves, ten inches across, and huge trusses of golden yellow flowers.

(Above left) *Lysichitum americanum*, the Yellow Skunk Cabbage.

(Above right) *Menyanthes trifoliata*, the Bog or Buck Bean.

(Left) *Pontederia cordata*, the Pickerel Weed.

me as a relatively unscientific horticulturist they are distinct, the centre of the flowers of *S. sagittifolia* being black and crimson and those of *S. japonica* yellow. Certainly if one orders plants from a nurseryman this is how they will be classified. There is also a very fine double form 'Flore Pleno' with flowers like tiny white powder puffs.

All the popular varieties have ribbon-like submerged foliage and long stemmed arrow-like aerial leaves which in deep water will often float. All arise from leafy sheaths at the base of the plant, together with the flower spike which bears the tiered whorls of tri-petalled blooms.

Apart from the two kinds mentioned previously, the only other species common to cultivation is *S. latifolia*, and this for its imposing stature rather than its ornamental value. Under favourable conditions in slightly acid mud, this splendid plant is capable of attaining a height of four or five feet, with handsome soft green awl-shaped leaves and sprays of snow white flowers. Many different forms have been described, but those most likely to be encountered are *S. latifolia var. pubescens*, with hairy foliage, and *S. latifolia* 'Flore Pleno' with double flowers. Propagation is by collecting the winter buds and planting them separately.

SAURURUS   Lizards' Tail

The common Lizards' Tail, *Saururus cernuus*, (syn. *S. lucidus*) is a rather bizarre, but nevertheless attractive aquatic plant for shallow water. It produces clumps of heart-shaped foliage, which often assume bronze autumnal tints and quaint nodding terminal sprays of creamy-white flowers during July and August. A variety called *S. loureiri* has been known to cultivation, but I have never seen this. Apparently it is of Chinese origin and has paler foliage and erect rather than nodding sprays of flowers. Propagation of both is by division.

SCIRPUS   Bulrush

The Scirpus, or now more correctly *Schoenoplectus*, are represented by about twenty-five species well distributed in the northern hemisphere, the most common being *S. lacustris*, the Bulrush in which the infant Moses was said to have been cradled.

This is an extremely useful plant for shallow water, with stiff dark-green needle-like leaves arising from short hard creeping rhizomes. During June and July the foliage is crowned with pendant tassels of crowded reddish-brown flowers followed by clusters of insignificant triangular fruits.

A close companion, *S. tabernaemontani*, the Glaucous Bulrush, looks very much like a superior form of *S. lacustris* and should be grown in preference whenever possible. Its slender foliage is steely-grey with a conspicuous mealy bloom, and bedecked with terminal sprays of small dark brown flowers.

Although a garden-worthy plant in its own right, *S. tabernaemontani* has given rise to the outstanding Zebra Rush, *S. t.* 'Zebrinus', a very popular and widely commercialised mutant with stems that are alternately barred green and white. This rarely grows above 3 ft high, doubtless restricted to some extent by the lack of chlorophyll in the white bands and thrives best when allowed to colonise very shallow water. Unfortunately, plain green stems are sometimes produced and these should be removed at source, as they will rapidly outgrow the desirable variegated portion if allowed to remain.

Apart from the Zebra Rush, the only other commonly cultivated bulrush is *S. tabernaemontani* 'Albescens', a handsome plant of uncertain origin, said by some to be a separate species in its own right, yet considered by others to be a hybrid of unknown parentage. Its stout upright stems are a glowing sulphurous-white conspicuously marked with thin green longitudinal stripes. These arise in clumps from thick creeping rhizomes which are frost-tender and should be protected from the vagaries of our winter climate with a layer of straw. Propagation of all the varieties is by division of the clumps shortly after they start to sprout.

SPARGANIUM Bur Reed
The common Bur Reed, *Sparganium ramosum*, is a rather coarse rush-like plant which produces fresh green foliage and clustered heads of brownish-green flowers. These leave a somewhat spiky looking seed head rather reminiscent of an extremely diminutive teasel. In the small pool the Bur Reed is seldom worth contemplat-

ing especially if the pool is made with a liner, as the creeping rootstocks easily pierce and ruin it if made of polythene. However, in large expanses of water, especially where ducks are encouraged, it is of great value. Propagation is by division and separating of the creeping rootstock.

TRIGLOCHIN   Arrowgrass
The native Marsh Arrowgrass, *Triglochin palustris*, is a plant of dubious merit for the shallow margins of a small pool. It produces crowded tufts of slender succulent foliage about a foot high and terminal spikes of greenish-white flowers. Although many people welcome it to their pool, I would not unreservedly recommend its inclusion as it is of somewhat drab appearance and spreads rather rapidly by seed.

TYPHA   Reedmace
The Reedmaces are probably the most familiar and popular rushes of all. Often erroneously referred to as 'bulrushes', these are the plants whose thick brown poker-like fruiting heads are dyed by florists for winter decoration.

Two common native species, *T. angustifolia* and *T. latifolia*, although very impressive when growing along streamsides and around large ponds, should be regarded with caution when contemplated for the garden pool, for they attain a height of six or seven feet and spread rapidly by means of thick white rhizomes, soon becoming an embarrassment if not severely restrained.

A similar species known as *T. truxillensis* from the southern United States is occasionally grown in this country, but cannot be said to be reliably hardy. It is a giant of a plant, larger than either of the previous species, and resembling *T. angustifolia* in all but the minutest of botanical details.

Typha laxmannii (syn. T. stenophylla) and the diminutive Japanese *T. minima*, are by far the most desirable species for the average garden pool. Both possess an air of grace and dignity not encountered in any other genus of hardy aquatics and are less invasive. *Typha laxmannii* grows to a height of some three or four feet with slender willowy leaves and characteristic well proportioned flower heads, whereas *T. minima* rarely exceeds eighteen inches and produces masses of short fat brown flower spikes amidst a waving sea of grassy foliage. As with all Typha species these will grow happily in either moist soil or up to a foot of water, and both propagate readily by division.

VERONICA Brooklime

The only truly aquatic member of this very popular genus is *V. beccabunga*. Like many of its terrestrial cousins it has dark blue flowers with a white eye. But here the similarity ends, for these are not borne in familiar terminal spikes but in the axils of the leaves of trailing procumbent stems. Veronica, although not a spectacular plant, has many uses and is invaluable for climbing out of the water and masking the area where pool meets land. It will also spread across the surface of the water, providing shade for the fish and its hanging roots a suitable deposition for spawn. Propagation, which should be undertaken annually in the spring, is by stem cuttings about three inches long pushed into the mud or a tray of wet soil.

ZIZANIA Canadian Wild Rice

I was in rather a quandary as to whether to include the two cultivated species of Zizania, as neither are by any stretch of the imagination in any way decorative. However, as many people grow them in order to attract ducks and similar wild water birds to feed on their grain, I decided they must be included. The taller and more popular species is *Z. aquatica*, a North American native with slender arching reed-like foliage some eight or ten feet high. Its Siberian cousin, *Z. latifolia*, is of more modest stature, a mere four feet tall, but is a perennial and more permanent inhabitant. Propagation of *Z. aquatica* is by seed sown each spring and *Z. latifolia* by seed or division of the creeping rootstock.

FLOATING PLANTS

Floating aquatics in co-operation with submerged oxygenating plants perform a leading role in the maintenance of clear water in the garden pool. For not only do they compete with lower forms of plant life for the mineral salts in the water, but provide surface shade, which makes life intolerable for algae that attempt to dwell beneath them.

It is generally advised that at least one third of the total surface area of the pool, excluding the shallow marginal shelves, should be clothed in foliage if a correct balance is to exist. This need not necessarily be composed entirely of floating plants, as it will be readily appreciated that waterlilies will themselves make a considerable contribution in this direction with their floating lily pads.

AZOLLA Fairy Moss

The Fairy Mosses are floating subjects that are much in favour with aquarists for tropical aquaria and for this reason often considered to be tender by the newcomer to water gardening. However, at least two species, *Azolla caroliniana* and *A. filiculoides*, have proved to be completely hardy and have both become naturalised in ponds and ditches in many parts of the British Isles. Both look identical and, indeed, are only separable under a microscope.

Contrary to popular belief these plants belong to the Pteridophyta or fern family, a fact difficult for the layman to appreciate when confronted with the thick lacy carpet of floating bluish-green or, in the autumn, brilliant crimson congested foliage, for the first time.

Although hardy it is desirable to keep a portion of these plants in a frost-free place during the winter months, for when left outside they often form over-wintering bodies which fall to the bottom of the pool and do not return to the surface until the following summer when the water has become warmer. This is often too late for them to act as effective surface cover, whereas a portion of the plant that has been kept actively growing, introduced into the pool, will spread quickly during late April and have the desired effect.

HYDROCHARIS Frogbit

The Frogbit, *Hydrocharis morsus-ranae*, is a close relative of that other popular floating aquatic the Water Soldier, *Stratiotes aloides*. First glances give no hint of its close botanical affinity, as its floating leaves are kidney shaped and arranged in rosettes around fleshy nodes. The white three-petalled flowers are the give-away, for they appear to be identical except for a yellow spot at the base of each petal.

In common with many other aquatics, the Frogbit forms turions in which to over-winter. These sink to the bottom of the pool during late September and reappear again about the middle of May, for which reason again it is advisable to remove a few plants to sheltered quarters, to be started into growth early in the spring in the manner prescribed for Azolla.

LEMNA Duckweed

Although useful green food for fish the Duckweeds, with the exception of the Ivy Duckweed *Lemna trisulca*, cannot be considered as suitable additions to the garden pool as they spread very rapidly and soon entirely obscure the water from view. The more amenable Ivy Duckweed is a dark-green crispy foliage plant which does not float completely on the surface as do the other duckweeds, but just beneath. It produces minute greenish flowers of no significance, being principally grown for its foliage effect.

STRATIOTES Water Soldier

The Water Soldier, *Stratiotes aloides*, is a widely distributed native of Europe and north-west Asia and produces dense rosettes of dark green spiny leaves reminiscent of a pineapple top. Its creamy-white flowers, which may be male, female or hermaphrodite, are produced throughout late summer either solitarily from the leaf axils (female) or in clusters in a pinkish papery spathe (male). In this country they have no bearing on the rate of reproduction as fruits are rarely if ever formed. But this is of little consequence, for young plants are borne in profusion on the long wiry stolons which issue from the swollen leaf bases of adult plants.

TRAPA Water Chestnut

Trapa natans is a handsome little fellow with rosettes of dark green rhomboidal floating leaves and unusual creamy-white axillary blooms. Although it is technically an annual, the hard black-horned 'nuts' which are produced in abundance throughout late summer, germinate very freely and provide the gardener with an ample supply of fresh plants each spring. The seeds, which are about the size of a chestnut, contain starchy material and are sold widely for food in southern Europe.

Many people consider the Water Chestnut to be unreliably hardy in this country, yet I have over-wintered it quite successfully here in a comparatively cold area of East Anglia. Those believing it to be tender generally collect the 'nuts' before winter sets in and store them in a bowl or jar of water in a cool yet frost-free place. It must be emphasised that on no account should the seeds be allowed to dry out as they will invariably perish. There is also no point in attempting to germinate them after one season, as recent research has proved beyond all reasonable doubt that viability is lost after as short a period as six months.

UTRICULARIA Bladderworts

The bladderworts are probably the most unusual and botanically fascinating genus of rootless floating plants. As with *Lemna trisulca*, described earlier, they are submerged floating plants rather than surface floating plants. Their leaves are divided into segments bearing small bladders which trap all manner of aquatic insect life, which is subsequently decomposed and absorbed as an additional source of food. Utricularia is a cosmopolitan genus of some two hundred species of which no more than eight are hardy in the British Isles.

Our native Greater Bladderwort, *Utricularia vulgaris*, is the one commonly offered commercially and, to my mind, the most showy of the hardy species. During July it produces striking golden yellow flowers on slender spikes some six inches above the water. They look superficially like those of an antirrhinum, but are more sparsely distributed along the flower spike.

Several forms which differ very slightly from the true species are known to botanists; notably the north American *U. vulgaris var. americana*, a plant of more robust growth and with much narrower flower spurs than those of the common species.

The Western Bladderwort, *U. neglecta*, is generally considered to be part of the same complex as *U. vulgaris*. This has leaf segments almost totally devoid of bristles and the lower lip of each flower clearly flattened. It is interesting to note that the bladders only develop on the bright green foliage whereas in *U. vulgaris* they are borne on both green and colourless foliage.

Conversely with the Intermediate Bladderwort, *U. intermedia*, bladders are borne on the colourless leaves and seldom on the bright green extensively dissected foliage. Unlike other hardy species the colourless lower portion often becomes anchored to the mud and although never producing true roots, the plant ceases to be free-floating and becomes a deep water aquatic. Between July and September short spikes of sulphur-yellow flowers streaked with deep mahogany-red are produced from amidst the tangled mass of fresh green floating leaves.

The north American *U. inflata* is probably the curio of this very interesting family, for beneath each raceme of flowers is a dense whorl of inflated branches which seemingly gives the plant additional buoyancy. The flowers are unfortunately not as attractive as those of any other species, but the plant is well worth acquiring for its curiosity value alone.

Similarly our native Lesser Bladderwort, *U. minor*, has relatively insignificant blooms, but what it lacks in quality it makes up for in quantity and when in full bloom a sizeable, well-established plant makes a truly magnificent picture. The individual spikes are almost wand-like and bear tiny pouched flowers of soft primrose, while the olive-green foliage is delicate and lacy and interspersed with relatively large dark green bladders.

WOLFFIA

Wolffia arrhiza is a plant of absolutely no horticultural merit or distinction and not worthy of mention were it not for the fact that it is our smallest native flowering plant and therefore worthy of inclusion as a conversation piece. Formerly included as a duck-weed under the name of *Lemna arrhiza*, it was eventually allocated a genus of its own following the discovery that it always remains rootless.

It grows in dense floating masses, each plant consisting of a tiny green globular or ovoid thallus no more than one millimetre across, which remains in character throughout the year despite the fact that it may sink to the bottom or become inexplicably suspended half way between there and the surface during the winter months.

SUBMERGED OXYGENATING PLANTS

Submerged oxygenating plants are essential for creating and maintaining a correct balance in the garden pool for not only do they replace the oxygen lost to respiration, but compete with lower forms of plant life for mineral salts, thereby preventing the water becoming green and 'thick' with slimes and algae.

On being received from the nursery, oxygenating plants may give cause for some alarm for they will appear to be merely a bunch of rootless cuttings held together with a strip of lead around the base. However, once introduced into the pool roots are rapidly initiated and the cuttings soon form a sizeable clump.

When planting submerged plants, do not merely throw them into water as is often recommended, for whilst it is true that the plants gain most of their nourishment directly from the water, they cannot become established successfully unless anchored to the bottom. In well-established pools with an accumulation of mulm on the floor this method of dropping the plants into the water and allowing the lead weight to take them root down to the bottom does have some measure of success, but it should not be practised in preference to conventional planting methods.

Although submerged plants require anchoring to the bottom, it does not follow that they require a huge pot or basket of earth in which to become established. A small flower pot for a single bunch or a plastic seed tray for half a dozen bunches is adequate. The rooting medium can be merely fine stones, although they generally grow more vigorously and successfully in a heavy loam soil topped off with a layer of pea shingle to discourage the burrowings of fish.

But no matter which medium or container is used, there is one important thing to remember when planting any bunched oxygenating subjects and that is to bury the lead strip, for if left exposed it often rots through the stems of the cuttings which then come floating to the top.

Stocking rate to ensure relatively clear water from the word go is usually recommended as one bunch to every two square feet of surface area, excluding the shallow marginal shelves, although this can be varied slightly with the variety involved and to a certain extent according to the expanse of water to be stocked.

APIUM   Water Celery

The Water Celery, *Apium inundatum*, is an attractive fresh green plant with delicate fern-like foliage and crowded heads of small white flowers above water level. A species sometimes offered, *A. nodiflorum*, is similar but weedy and quite invasive.

CALLITRICHE   Starwort

The Starworts, although inclined to be temperamental, are extremely useful additions to a pool, for their luxuriant cress-like foliage is loved by goldfish and provides the necessary green material in their diet.

By far the most popular are *Callitriche platycarpa* and *C. hermaphroditica*, the latter sometimes known as the Autumnal Starwort. More commonly known by their old names *C. verna* and *C. autumnalis* respectively, these two useful species readily establish themselves in shallow water near the margins. Both look similar in outward appearance, having small fresh green narrowly elliptical leaves in dense terminal whorls, but *C. platycarpa* will be seen to produce rosettes of broadly elliptical floating leaves, whereas *C. hermaphroditica* remains completely submerged. The latter, however, does have the advantage of remaining evergreen.

Callitriche stagnalis, an attractive inhabitant of ponds and ditches throughout the British Isles, does not seem reliably perennial under cultivation; its oval leaves often disappear as soon as fruiting has taken place, but it must be included here as it is a fairly common species to be offered commercially.

A species barely distinguishable from *C. stagnalis* in the early stages of growth is *C. obtusangula*, but any fear of confusion is soon allayed when the dense clusters of handsome rhomboidal floating leaves appear.

A rare but improved hybrid form *C.C. lachii (C. obtusangula* × *C. intermedia)* is far superior, but difficulty may be experienced in obtaining a specimen. Its floating leaves exhibit the characteristics of *C. obtusangula*, being almost diamond shaped, whilst the submerged foliage is long and narrow like that of *C. intermedia*.

CERATOPHYLLUM   Hornwort
The Hornworts are particularly useful subjects for difficult ponds, preferring to inhabit the lower depths, particularly where it is cold or partially shaded. They all have dark-green bristly foliage arranged in dense whorls around slender brittle stems. In early spring these are rooted to the pool floor, but as the summer advances they float to the surface, the stem towards the terminal buds thickening and breaking off, leaving the upper portions to sink to the bottom as turions or winter buds.

Ten species are known to botanists, but only *Ceratophyllum demersum* and *C. submersum* are at all common in cultivation and these to the average gardener will appear alike; the differences being of a minor botanical nature.

CHARA   Stonewort
Although only occasionally introduced to the pool deliberately as an oxygenating plant, they often find their own way in naturally. Loosely speaking they are an intermediate between the higher submerged plants and filamentous algae, being of a thick hairy appearance, but rooting strongly to the pool floor. They vary in colour from light green to bluish green and all possess an offensive odour if handled, akin to that commonly attributed to cats. Apart from oxygenating properties they also have the virtue of extracting lime from the water and if a plant is removed from the pool and allowed to dry out in the sun, one will notice that it is thickly coated in a chalky deposit. Many species are known to science and any of the native ones could appear in the pond, but the one that is occasionally bunched and sold as an oxygenating plant is *Chara aspera*.

ELEOCHARIS   Hair Grass
The common Hair Grass, *Eleocharis acicularis*, is a very fine oxygenating plant that is admirably suited to the pool, no matter what size, for it spreads politely and carpets the pool floor never

interfering with the fish or decorative plants. When well-established it looks like underwater seedling grass, but is in fact more closely related to the sedges. A number of different species are grown at times by aquarists, but it is only *E. acicularis* that can be unreservedly recommended for the pool.

ELODEA Water Thyme

The Water Thymes are probably the most familiar hardy submerged oxygenating plants and are generally acknowledged as being the best oxygenators. Unfortunately nomenclature has always been muddled, and it is only during recent years that they have been disentangled and reclassified as Elodea, Egeria and Lagarosiphon respectively. Many old books and still some nursery catalogues refer to all three genera as Anacharis.

About ten species, all of American origin, are currently known as Elodea, the commonest being the Canadian Pondweed, *Elodea canadensis*. This is the plant introduced into Europe at the end of the last century, which spread rapidly along canals and waterways making them virtually unnavigable. Fortunately it died out after several years, leaving a much less pernicious form in its place. It is believed by some authorities that the plant originally introduced was the male form separated botanically at that time as *E. planchonii*, a plant now rare in cultivation, and the *E. canadensis* now common in these regions is the female form. The species is typified by dark green serrulate or curved lance-like leaves borne in whorls around long branching stems and tiny floating lilac flowers with trailing thread-like stalks. In large expanses of water it often proves difficult to control, but under average garden pool conditions where any excess of underwater growth can easily be curtailed, it is an investment.

Few of the other true Elodeas are commonly offered as pond plants, as none can compete with *E. canadensis* for vigour, ease of cultivation, or indeed hardiness. But one may come across either *E. callitrichoides* or *E. nuttallii* (syn. *Hydrilla verticillata*) in the catalogue of an aquarists' supplier and the keen pond-keeper may well think these worthy of a trial, despite the latter's notorious dislike of acidic water or organic matter in the rooting medium.

FONTINALIS Willow Moss
The common Willow Moss, *Fontinalis antipyretica*, a handsome
evergreen native with dark-green mossy foliage is most adaptable,
thriving equally well in sun or shade, but preferring slightly moving
acid water. It is said that it was the dried foliage of this species
which was formerly used by Scandinavians to pack between walls
and chimneys in their wooden houses to exclude air and thereby
reduce the risk of fire. Together with the more diminutive, but
nevertheless most desirable, *F. gracilis*, it makes an admirable
spawning ground for fish.

HOTTONIA Water Violet
The Hottonias are excellent oxygenating plants but rather temperamental under cultivation. They have handsome whorled submerged
leaves and fine upstanding flower spikes. Two species are known,
both of which form turions that sink to the mud during the winter
months. The most popular and easily obtainable is our native,
Hottonia palustris, with pale green foliage and spikes of lilac or
whitish flowers. Its rare and curious North American cousin, *H.
inflata*, is almost identical except that its branched flower stems are
grotesquely inflated.

ISOETES Quillwort
Surprisingly members of the Pteridophyta or fern family, the
various species of quillworts are exceedingly useful oxygenating
plants, especially in water that has a tendency towards acidity.
Only one species is commonly commercially available and this is
our native *Isoetes lacustris*, a sturdy little plant with dark-olive
green quill-like leaves, which arise from a circular brown corm.
Under natural conditions the leaves often attain a length of some
eight or ten inches, but in the average pool will rarely exceed four
inches in height and will stand firm and erect like very stout
porcupine quills.

   In addition to the true species there is a large and most desirable
variant *I. lacustris var. Morei* which has flaccid leaves some one and
a half to two feet long.

LAGAROSIPHON

Lagarosiphon major, or the *Elodea crispa* of commerce, is a very adaptable plant thriving in the most unlikely of places and thrusting up long succulent stems densely clothed in broad dark-green crispy foliage. This is probably the finest of all oxygenating plants as it rarely gets out of hand and retains its character throughout the year.

LOBELIA

Although related to the popular bedding Lobelia, the appearance of *L. dortmanna* does not belie its close affinity. It forms carpets of erect blunt foliage from which arise a profusion of wiry stems with terminal clusters of lavender coloured blooms. Propagation by division.

MYRIOPHYLLUM   Milfoil

There are forty-five known species of *Myriophyllum*, but only two which are commonly grown as submerged oxygenating plants; the Spiked Milfoil *Myriophyllum spicatum*, and the Whorled Milfoil *M. verticillatum*. Both have long trailing stems which support dense whorls of narrow submerged leaves, and spikes of small, yet not unattractive flowers. In *M. verticillatum* these are crowded together around a thickened spike, the male ones having curious yellowish-green petals, whilst the females remain completely naked. Similarly with *M. spicatum* the female flowers are almost devoid of petals, whereas the male ones are bright crimson and very striking.

Several other species creep into cultivation from time to time, but differ little in habit and appearance and are probably only of interest to the botanist. But should the opportunity arise of obtaining a plant of the North American *M. farewellii*, it should be grasped with both hands, for this handsome species produces dense forests of lush green underwater growth that provides a haven for spawning fish.

OENANTHE   Water Dropwort

Oenanthe fluviatilis is a not uncommonly offered oxygenating plant with dense carrot-like foliage and umbels of indifferent white flowers. Where space is not at a premium it is a plant of great value and considerable beauty, its lush green underwater foliage swaying most majestically in the water, but where space is restricted it is best avoided.

POTAMOGETON Pondweed
The Potamogetons are a large and valuable family of plants which for practical purposes has been split into two sub-tribes; the true Potamogetons and the Coleogeton. The former consists of those species sometimes producing floating leaves and which are wind pollinated, the latter containing those completely submerged and water pollinated.

Of the Coleogeton only two are at all common as pond plants: these are the Slender-leaved Pondweed, *P. filiformis*, and the Fennel-leaved Pondweed, *P. pectinatus*. Both at first glance seem very much alike, but closer examination will reveal that the foliage of the latter is much more branched and the fruit, although larger, is not so prominently beaked. Once established *P. pectinatus* can become invasive, crowding out other less vigorous and more choice aquatics; so *P. filiformis* should be grown in preference wherever possible.

The most familiar of the true Potamogetons is the Curled Pond-weed, *P. crispus*. With its handsome serrated and undulating bronze-green translucent leaves, it makes a wonderful addition to any pool. Its flowers are also quite significant, being held above the water on short stout spikes; they are deep crimson with creamy-white interiors. Several species somewhat resembling the Curled Pondweed, but lacking the attractive crinkled margins to the leaves are sometimes encountered, especially the Sharp-leafed Pondweed *P. acutifolius*, and Grass-Wrack Pondweed *P. compressus*. Both have distinctive flattened leaf stems, but the latter is further distinguished by its large toothed greenish-brown fruits.

Several of the larger species of Potamogeton produce handsome floating leaves and some of these, if kept within bounds, will make a useful addition to the outdoor pool. The Bog Pondweed, *P. poly-gonifolius*, and Various-leafed Pondweed *P. gramineus*, are the most amenable kinds. The former produce quaint elliptical floating leaves and dense spikes of greenish fruits, whereas the latter has almost oblong floating leaves and exceedingly attractive broad, lanceolate submerged foliage. Unfortunately, *P. polygonifolius* will only grow in acid water, so for those inflicted with a pool that has a relatively high lime content it is better to try the Fen Pondweed *P. coloratus*, a species that will thrive under these conditions. The floating leaves of this plant are almost identical to those of the Bog Pondweed, but its translucent under-water foliage exhibits a pronounced veining, which to my mind makes it a much more desirable acquisition.

Beautiful veining is also the principal attribute of the Loddon Pondweed *P. nodosus*, both the floating and submerged foliage being etched with a tracery of slender black lines. The fine upstanding spikes of fruits also give the plant a distinctive air, but unfortunately many of these are abortive and as far as I am aware no hybrids have resulted from a union with this plant. This seems regrettable, as the superb veining of this species infused into some of the better leafed varieties such as the Reddish Pondweed *P. alpinus* would result in a most interesting and desirable race of aquatics.

Few other species with floating leaves are of any value to the pond-keeper, even if readily available, for they will invariably swamp the pond in a very short time. Two good examples of this are the Floating Pondweed *P. natans* and the Shining Pondweed *P. lucens*, both despite having most striking foliage, quickly outgrow their allocated space and become a continual nuisance.

Of the innumerable natural hybrids of Potamogeton, only two are sufficiently distinct as to be worthy of special mention. *Potamogeton* × *zizii (P. lucens* × *P. gramineus)* and *P.* × *salicifolius (P. lucens* × *P. perfoliatus)* both of which have effectively reduced the vigorous and often undesirable *P. lucens* to manageable proportions.

RANUNCULUS Crowfoot
Of the multiplicity of Crowfoots known to botanists, it is *Ranunculus aquatilis* that is usually dubbed the Water Crowfoot on account of its flaccid deeply dissected submerged foliage which closely resembles an outstretched bird's foot. The floating leaves which succeed these during mid-summer are dark green, deeply lobed and not unlike those of a normal terrestrial species. They are crowned

in June with an outstanding display of glistening white and golden blooms.

Many other species are often sold under the collective name of Water Crowfoot or *R. aquatilis* by water plant nurseries. As stocks have nearly always been originally derived from native plants, they are often muddled and the observant gardener may well be able to pick out several different choice and distinctive species. Indeed, more often than not, I have been sent plants of *R. peltatus* as *R. aquatilis*. I might add it was to my advantage, for these produce even larger cream and yellow flowers above lush rounded floating foliage. A smaller leaved, but equally large flowering sort, *R. aquatilis var. floribundus* may also be encountered and this is an even more desirable acquisition.

TILLAEA

Until recent years these plants were relatively unknown. However, the handsome Tillaea (or should we more correctly say *Crassula?*) *recurva* has become very popular, being a very fine oxygenating subject comparable at least with *Lagarosiphon major*. Its foliage is of a fine hard, cress-like nature and during summer is decorated with tiny white axillary flowers. If planted in a pool that is persistently green, in thick well-rooted clumps, it can be almost guaranteed to clear the water within three or four weeks. My favourite, and certainly a very useful and adaptable plant.

(5)

Bog Garden Plants

ACONITUM Monkshood
The common Monkshood of the old-fashioned cottage garden, *Aconitum napellus*, is known to the majority of people. Of somewhat Delphinium-like appearance, with erect spikes of hooded navy blue flowers some five feet high, the monkshood is a distinctive member of the bog garden. While it is true that this and many other varieties of Aconitum can be grown in the ordinary border, it is also true to say that the blooms and foliage produced there pale into insignificance when compared with the magnificence of a specimen grown under conditions of continuous moisture.

Apart from the well-known species there is a bi-coloured—blue and white—kind called appropriately enough *A.n. bicolor*, and a dwarf stocky deep blue variety which seldom exceeds two feet in height called '*Bressingham Spire*'. *Aconitum wilsonnii* and its cultivar '*Barker's Variety*' are a complete contrast, growing five or six feet high and, surprisingly, flowering in the autumn, at least three months after their cousins.

Aconitum lycoctonum is unusual in so far as it has yellow flowers, but the best form is *var. pyrenaicum*, a compact fellow with large hooded flowers. However, the real surprise in this genus is the occurrence of a climbing species from Siberia, *A. volubile*. If given a twiggy support or small shrub amidst which to scramble this gangling character makes a brave show. Propagation by seed or division.

AJUGA Bugle
The various species of this family of dwarf creeping plants are invaluable in growing from the ground surrounding the pool so

that they can tumble over the edge to disguise its harshness. The common *Ajuga reptans* can be a bit of a nuisance, but its varieties 'Purpurea' with purplish-bronze leaves and the pinkish-buff and cream variegated 'Multicolor' are not at all invasive and carpet the ground with foliage of excellent substance. *Ajuga pyramidalis* has plain green leaves, but is outstanding for its substantial spikes of gentian blue flowers which pale the drab navy blue ones of the previous kinds into insignificance.

Ajuga genevensis is often recommended for pool-side planting, but it is not a plant for the bog garden, rather is it a plant to allow to spread from the drier reaches of the ordinary garden up to the pool. Unlike its comrades it does not grow from runners, but just spreads outwards in the course of living. Its flowers are blue or occasionally white or pink and borne in spikes during early summer. Propagation by runners and division.

ANEMONE Windflower

Two species of Anemone can be grown in the bog garden, indeed *A. virginiana* can even stand periodic flooding. If left to its own devices it soon forms clumps of hairy leaves on three foot stems and bears clusters of greenish-white flowers throughout the summer. Its colleague *A. rivularis* is, in my opinion, much finer, producing loose umbels of snow-white flowers filled in the centre with bright violet anthers. Propagation by seed or division.

ANTHERICUM

A beautiful genus of summer flowering perennials with tufts of narrow grassy foliage from which arise numerous slender spikes of pure white flowers. *Anthericum liliago*, the St. Bernard's lily, and *A. liliastrum major*, the St. Bruno lily, are the most readily obtainable. Both possess grassy foliage and two foot high spikes of white flowers, the difference between them lying merely in the fact that the individual blooms of *A. liliastrum major* are much larger and of a bold trumpet shape. Propagation by seed or division.

ARUNCUS Goat's Beard

There are few cottage gardens that do not possess at least one clump of Goat's Beard, known amongst gardeners variously as *Spiraea aruncus, Aruncus sylvester* and now for what I hope will be the last change, *A. dioicus*. It is a tall handsome plant of Astilbe-like appearance, carrying waving plumes of creamy-white. The leaves are the palest green and deeply cut and lobed, while the stems are hard and green and of similar appearance to bamboo. A dwarf form seldom exceeding three feet in height is 'Kneiffi' which is otherwise of identical character and much more suitable for the smaller garden of today. Propagation by division.

ARUNDO   Giant Reed

Anyone who has visited southern Europe will have seen this tall striking reed. The roadsides of southern France around the Rhone delta in the swampy area known as the Camargue are solid with hedges, living barriers, or whatever they might be called of this amazing giant reed. In this country, however, one cannot rely upon *Arundo donax*, as the common variety is known, to be absolutely hardy. However, when well-established and growing strongly it is a magnificent sight, its sugar-cane-like appearance giving an air of tropical luxuriance to the most traditional of gardens. In its natural habitat it attains a height of some twenty or so feet but in this country barely reaches eight. There is also a slightly shorter growing cultivar with cream and green striped foliage, 'Variegata'. Propagation by division.

ASCLEPIAS   Milkweed

Asclepias incarnata, the Swamp Milkweed, is a splendid subject for moist areas near a natural pond or where there is sufficient space around an artificial one. Its only requirements are sunshine and abundant moisture and then it will produce stout leafy stems and crowded heads of rose coloured flowers. Apart from the ordinary variety, there is a kind with white flowers known as *A.i. var. alba*. Propagation by division in the spring.

ASTER

Everyone knows the bedding Asters and most folk know that Michaelmas Daisies are also Asters. Few, however, have ever seen or heard of the Swamp Aster *A. puniceus*, which seems a great shame, as with its rigid red stems some three feet high and crowded heads of small lilac flowers it is a most welcome addition to the bog garden. Propagation by seed or division.

ASTILBE   False Goat's Beard

All members of this attractive family flourish in a moist situation in sun or shade and produce clumps of handsome pale green foliage surmounted by dense feathery spikes of flowers. The popular hybrids of today are the result of unions between various Asiatic species such as *A. astilboides, A. japonica, A. sinensis* and *A. thunbergii.* None of these are in general cultivation as they produce relatively sparse and untidy flower spikes, but the hybrids they have sired are numerous. To take three good popular examples to cover the colour range, we have 'Fanal' which is bright crimson, 'White Gloria' obviously white, and the delicious salmon-pink 'Peach Blossom'. These and any of the other widely commercialised varieties make bold splashes of colour when planted in groups of six or eight and if one is to study any reputable grower's catalogue, suitable varieties combining the desired heights and colours can easily be selected. They generally flower during what one might term late summer, but the keen gardener may be interested to know that they force very easily in a cool greenhouse and make excellent spring pot plants.

For the pond-owner with a rock garden pool or very tiny pond, there are two varieties that are of a stature in keeping with such a feature and these are the *Astilbe crispa* cultivars 'Lilliput' and 'Perkeo'. Both have congested tufts of dark crinkled foliage, the former producing spires of tightly packed salmon-pink flowers and the latter blooms of an intense deep pink and neither exceeding a height of six inches even under ideal conditions. A slightly taller kind which generally reaches a foot or so in height, *A. sinensis* 'Pumila', has prostrate tufts of dark green foliage from which stout spikes of rosy-purple flowers are produced. All are readily propagated by division.

BUPTHALMUM

A coarse straggling genus of daisy-like plants of which the yellow flowering *B. salicifolium* is well-known to those with herbaceous borders. However, there is a much larger moisture loving species,

B. speciosum, with hairy aromatic foliage and large drooping yellow daisy flowers. As this plant generally attains a height of some three or four feet and maybe as much through, it can only be considered as suitable for the streamside or beside a large pool. Propagation is by seed or division.

CARDAMINE   Cuckoo Flower

A pretty genus of spring flowering waterside perennials easily grown in sun or partial shade, but only our native *C. pratensis* and its very showy double form *C. pratensis flore-plena*, are suitable for growing actually in boggy conditions. The latter is particularly fine, seldom exceeding six inches in height and producing close tufts of ferny foliage from which arise a number of slender stems with crowded spikes of double rosy-lilac flowers. Propagation by seed.

EUPATORIUM   Joe-Pye-Weed

This is a very useful genus of strong growing perennials forming bold bushes of dark-green foliage with crowded heads of flowers that are particularly useful for the larger bog garden or streamside planting. *Eupatorium ageratoides* or *E. fraseri* as it is more often known has dense heads of white flowers on two foot high stems, as does the slightly bolder *E. perfoliatum*. *Eupatorium cannabinum* is the variety with plum-coloured blooms in large terminal heads and *E. purpureum* is another four footer with crowded heads of purple flowers. Propagation by seed or division.

FILIPENDULA

Of the genus that once was known as Spiraea, those plants so allied that they resembled the common Meadow Sweet, *Filipendula ulmaria*, have been collected together and afforded the generic title Filipendula. The double form of *F. ulmaria* and the golden leafed variety 'Aurea' are particularly happy in wet conditions, as are the deep pink *F. purpurea* and the ferny leafed *F. hexapetala*. This is the plant normally referred to as Dropwort and, together with its double form 'flore-pleno', makes a bold show of ivory blossoms during mid-summer.

Two other Filipendulas are commonly available and these make a grand show when plenty of space is available. Even when not, they can provide a useful background of foliage and tasteful bloom for the smaller inhabitants of the average bog garden. *Filipendula rubra,* and particularly its much improved variety 'Magnifica', is superb with glistening spires of deep pink blooms that change with age to intense carmine-rose. Under favourable conditions these may be five feet high, quite a contrast to the delicately poised three foot stems of pale pink blooms produced by its cousin *F. palmata.* All the Filipendulas can be propagated by division and the true species by seed as well.

GUNNERA

Gunnera manicata is one of the largest and certainly most remarkable herbaceous plants that can be grown outside in this country. Although to the uninitiated it has the appearance of a giant rhubarb, closer inspection will reveal several differences. Its leaves are large, five to six feet or more across and more or less kidney-shaped. The margins are deeply indented and the undersides and leaf stalks are liberally sprinkled with unpleasant bristly hairs. The much branching flower spike is not exotic or spectacular, but curious; like a huge red-green bottle brush that may be anything between one and three feet high. It arises from a thick creeping rhizome that is densely clothed in brown papery scales, which during the winter months have been likened to a reclining bear.

Gunneras like a moist cool position in which to grow, the ideal situation from both an aesthetic and cultural point of view being alongside a stream where their huge spreading leaves can be mirrored in the rippling water, a position where moisture is plentiful but stagnation avoided. Winter protection in the north and exposed parts of Scotland is necessary and is also prudent in more southerly areas. A covering of straw or bracken or, with established plants, their own frost blackened leaves, is usually sufficient to prevent damage to the over-wintering buds.

Apart from *G. manicata,* there are several other rarer species including the similar slightly smaller *G. chilensis.* Other than in size, natural distribution and shape of rhizome and leaf, of which the latter is not particularly apparent, there is little to commend it in preference to the more readily available *G. manicata.* Propagation is by division of the crowns or by severing large growing points during late spring and planting these in a moist shady position. Seed sown immediately it ripens often results in a healthy crop of seedlings.

HEMEROCALLIS Day Lily
Although considered by most gardeners to be ordinary border perennials, the various varieties of Hemerocallis without exception do best in really wet ground. *Hemerocallis fulva* is the common kind and has surprisingly been in cultivation for nearly four hundred years. It is a vigorous plant some four feet high with orange and brown flowers four inches across. Two varieties of this 'Flore-pleno' and 'Kwanso Flore-pleno' are much improved, the latter being particularly fine with double blooms variegated with yellowish-green.

The modern Day Lily hybrids, of which there are nearly as many as there are roses, are of complex origin and descended from *H. fulva*, *H. lilio-asphodelus*, *H. flava* and the occasional intervention of *H. minor*, *H. serotina* and *H. aurantiaca*. This huge cauldron of genes has been stirred by hybridisers for many years particularly on the other side of the Atlantic so that there are now numerous very fine hybrids covering most of the yellow and red areas of the spectrum. Of all the kinds I have grown I like 'Hyperion' lemon yellow; 'Mikado' orange with a brown throat; 'Pink Charm'; 'Margaret Perry' which one might describe as Jaffa orange; the reddish-orange 'Tejas' and the deep velvety-mauve 'Black Prince'. Propagation by division.

HOSTA Plantain Lily
One cannot ever hope to disentangle the complex nomenclature of this splendidly colourful genera of hardy foliage plants, known originally as Funkia and with names and forms that are so close to one another, that the ordinary gardener cannot do better than follow the names given by reputable nurserymen and relate them to the plants they sell. Certainly this is the way I am dealing with them here. All species and cultivars are grown basically for their attractive plain or variegated foliage, although their pendant sprays of white or lilac flowers are not insignificant.

The commonest and most popular of the striped varieties is *H. undulata medio-variegata* with slightly twisted leaves in a complex mixture of cream, white and green. The hybrid 'Thomas Hogg' is a little more orderly with plain green leaves with just a white marginal band. This handsome fellow is a cultivar derived from the plain green *H. lancifolia*, itself a very worthwhile acquisition. It also gives rise to a golden leafed kind 'Aurea' and the very large 'Fortis'.

Hosta glauca, or as it is sometimes listed *H. sieboldii*, has glaucous leaves six inches wide and a foot long, while its variety 'Robusta' is even larger. The handsome *H. fortunei* is another plain foliage variety, particularly noted for its attractive spikes of funnel-shaped lilac flowers. Propagation of the species is by seed or division and the cultivars by division alone.

IRIS

Apart from the species of truly aquatic Iris described earlier, there are a multiplicity of species and varieties that do best in moist ground. These are so luxurious in their various shades of colour that one fails adequately to describe their charm and varied combinations. As with their totally aquatic neighbours they produce bold sheaves of grassy or sword-like foliage that is quite decorative amidst their flowers during June and July. They are quite at home when planted in bold masses on the sunny banks beside a pond or in single clumps in the bog garden where their roots can penetrate the water beneath.

Moisture-loving Irises immediately call to mind the Clematis Flowered Iris, *I. kaempferi*. When established they form strong tufts of broad grassy foliage surmounted by large clematis-like flowers, appearing as resplendent tropical butterflies at rest on the sombre foliage. Dozens of varieties of Japanese origin have been imported over the years, but the majority now have westernised names and are freely available. Some of the best varieties currently offered are 'Blue Heaven' rich purple-blue with a yellow throat; 'Hokkaido' pale blue lined and veined with maroon; 'Mandarin' deep purple-violet and 'Landscape at Dawn', lovely double blooms of pale rose-lavender.

Another useful group for similar situations is *Iris sibirica* and its hybrids. These have the same grassy foliage, and are possibly easier going, not resenting an alkaline soil as *Iris kaempferi* do. The sky blue variety 'Perry's Blue' is universally known, as are the purple 'Caesar' and the pure white 'Snow Queen'. 'Perry's Pigmy' is a dwarf growing kind of deep violet, while 'Ottawa' is of medium height and bright purple. 'Mrs. Saunders' has large flowers of dark blue reticulated with white and 'Emperor' is a fine large flowering kind of deep violet blue.

Apart from these two groups there are several species of similar disposition, but often not so readily available. *Iris aurea* is a robust species quite four feet high with flowers of deep golden yellow. *Iris bulleyana* is a small Chinese species with grassy foliage and delicate flowers of rich blue, similar in many ways to *I. setosa*, but lacking the lush broad foliage of that species. *Iris chrysographes* with deep purple flowers appreciates an open sunny position, while the giant white and yellow *I. ochroleuca* will tolerate anything as long as its roots are kept moist. Propagation of named varieties is by division, while the species can be reproduced from seed as well.

LIGULARIA

This is a genus which was formerly part of the vast Senecio 'empire' and contains those species which are herbaceous, moisture-loving, and with broad roughly heart-shaped leaves and huge mop heads or else erect spikes of droopy orange or yellow daisy-like flowers. In a moist situation they are magnificent but they must be kept permanently damp or else they wilt badly and become stunted and weedy.

The best-loved species is undoubtedly *L. clivorum*, with broad leaves and strong branching stems of bright orange flowers some four or five feet high, and with its improved cultivar forms such as the vivid 'Orange Queen', pale yellow flowered and purple-leafed 'Desdemona', and purplish leafed 'Othello', it makes a brave show during July and August. For the smaller garden 'Greynog Gold' with its bright golden flowers and diminutive stature is useful, but does not convey the same magnificence as its more substantial cousins. Unfortunately, *L. clivorum* and its varieties hybridise and seed very freely producing colonies of young plants with attractive foliage but, if allowed to develop, they form plants with straggly stems and mediocre flowers. The best policy with all Ligularia seedlings is to hoe them out immediately they are seen.

Apart from *L. clivorum* there are several other species which produce spikes of flowers as opposed to the characteristic mop heads. These flower from July until September and are particularly attractive when grouped with cultivars of *L. clivorum*. *Ligularia hessei* grows up to six feet high with spikes of glowing orange while *L. veitchiana* has heart-shaped leaves and blooms of golden yellow. *Ligularia wilsoniana* is a handsome large flowered species, slightly later but otherwise almost identical to *L. veitchiana*. Propagation is by division.

LOBELIA

Unlike the familiar bedding Lobelia, the perennial kinds are of upright spiky growth and revel in moist conditions. They are mostly hardy, although they appreciate protection from biting winds, especially during spring when young growth is emerging. *Lobelia cardinalis* and *L. fulgens* are the two best-known species, and hybrids from crosses between these two have always been popular, although perhaps not so latterly as in pre-war years. *Lobelia cardinalis* in its true form has plain green leaves and vivid red flowers, although in several commercial seed-raised strains the foliage is of a distinct purple or bronze shade. Indeed, the closely related *L. fulgens* with its beetroot-coloured stems and leaves, and bright red flowers are often mistakenly sold as *L. cardinalis*. Hybrids such as 'Queen Victoria' with very attractive maroon foliage and red flowers, 'Huntsman', brilliant scarlet, and 'Mrs. Humbert', flesh pink, embrace the characteristics of both and if grown from divisions are splendidly uniform. Both species and their cultivars grow to about three feet in height and flower throughout mid and late summer.

Lobelia × vedrariensis is a handsome hybrid of uncertain origin, absolutely hardy, and with tall spires of violet flowers and pea-green foliage splashed and bordered with maroon. Like all Lobelias it must have moisture and also appreciates shade when such is available. The smaller growing, *L. syphlitica*, with its dainty flowers of blue or white also likes the shade—indeed it tends to flag without it—but as the least impressive member of the genus, unless space abounds, I would not concern myself too much with it. All species can be propagated by seed or division and the named varieties by division alone.

LYSIMACHIA

There are a great number of species of Lysimachia known to cultivation, but the most useful to the water gardener is the Creeping Jenny, *L. nummularia*, and its golden leafed form 'Aurea'. This is a more or less evergreen carpeting plant that is ideal for masking the edge of a pool or providing an attractive ground cover between taller growing marsh plants in the bog garden. It seldom exceeds two inches in height and is studded with starry buttercup-like blooms during June and July.

Lysimachia punctata has similar flowers but these are borne in whorls up two foot high stems. It is an old-fashioned plant of somewhat coarse growth, but providing flowers for most of the summer. A similar kind, but with long drooping spikes of white flowers, is *L. clethroides*, and *L. vulgaris*, our native yellow loosestrife is another worth growing when space is not at a premium. Propagation is by seed, cuttings or division.

LYTHRUM   Loosestrife

There are only two species of Lythrum in general cultivation, but both, together with their cultivars, are well worth growing. *Lythrum salicaria* is our native Purple Loosestrife with stiff bushy stems four or five feet tall and slender spikes of deep rose-purple blooms. Improved garden varieties include 'The Beacon', 'Lady Sackville' and 'Robert' which cover the colour range from purple through rose-red to pink, the latter being particularly valuable owing to its neat and compact habit.

Lythrum virgatum is a smaller plant than *L. salicaria* and eminently suitable for the small modern garden. It has dark-green leaves and purple flowers and seldom exceeds two and a half feet in height. Varieties derived from *L. virgatum* are less inspiring than those from its more vigorous cousin, but 'Rose Queen' and 'Dropmore Purple' are well worth growing. Propagation is by seed for the species and cuttings taken during early spring of the named varieties.

PARNASSIA   Grass of Parnassus
The genus Parnassia contains several species of small growing marsh plants with close tufts of foliage and dainty white flowers on thin wiry stems. *Parnassia palustris* is the only species commonly grown, a very rare native with heart-shaped leaves and slender stems bearing snow-white flowers occasionally blotched with apple-green. It grows best in a damp peaty soil, preferably close to moving water such as a stream or cascade. Propagation by seed or division.

PELTIPHYLLUM   Umbrella Plant
Formerly known as *Saxifraga peltata*, but now as *Peltiphyllum peltatum*, this Californian native should find a home in any moderate size bog garden. Stout stems bear immense leaves of a bronzy-green hue which are often up to a foot in diameter. They are handsomely lobed and toothed and preceded in early spring by globular heads of rose coloured flowers on waving eighteen inch high stems. Propagation by seed or division of the fleshy rhizome.

PETASITES   Butterbur
Veritable giants for the waterside, the most popular and largest being *P. japonicus giganteus*. During early spring this produces a large crowded head of white flowers just above soil level long before the huge cabbagey leaves appear. These latter may attain a height of some four or five feet and look equally as impressive as those of Rheum or Gunnera. Propagation by seed or division.

PHORMIUM
The Phormiums are a genus of striking moisture-loving plants, somewhat unreliable in cold areas, but bringing a tropical air to gardens that are to their liking. *Phormium tenax*, the New Zealand Flax, is the one usually grown and has bold sword-like foliage of metallic green and stout stems bearing numerous curious red and yellow flowers. Its varieties *atropurpurea* with reddish-purple foliage and *variegata* with leaves of green, yellow and white are even more outstanding but much more difficult to acquire. A shorter

growing species similar in general appearance to *P. tenax* is sometimes offered by nurserymen and goes under the name of *P. cookianum* or more correctly *P. colensoi*. This is invaluable for the smaller garden, creating the same effect as its larger cousin, but without swamping its more diminutive neighbours. Propagation by seed or division.

PRIMULA

A genus of beautiful moisture-loving plants succeeding in sunny or partially shaded positions, and when planted in drifts present a picture of unrivalled splendour. They all form rosettes of distinctive foliage from which arise slender stems bearing richly coloured flowers arranged in globular heads or tiered whorls. The number of species available is legion, indeed one could devote a whole book to their description and cultivation and still not cover them comprehensively.

The earliest to flower are the popular Drumstick Primulas, *P. denticulata* and its forms. These bloom during March and April, producing rounded heads of blue or lilac flowers on short stout stems. The variety *alba* is white and *cashmireana* has lilac-purple blooms and mealy foliage.

Primula rosea and the improved cultivar 'Micia de Geer' flower at about the same time with a profusion of rose coloured blooms on six inch high stems above tufts of narrow foliage.

Primula aurantiaca is one of the first candelabra types to flower during early May, with tiers of bright orange blooms, while *P. bulleyana* is of similar coloration but with flowers that are larger and not produced until June or July. *Primula japonica* has crimson blooms in dense tiered whorls but is nowadays superseded by its cultivars 'Miller's Crimson' and 'Postford White', the latter which has taken over from the old-fashioned *P. japonica var. alba*. *Primula beesiana* and *P. burmanica* have flowers in shades of rosy and deep rosy-purple, while *P. pulverulenta* has magenta blooms on attractive mealy stems. A cultivar race known as 'Bartley Strain' has the same attractive stems but buff or pink flowers of considerable substance and is considered by many to be the finest of the moisture-loving Primulas.

Primula florindae and *P. sikkimensis* are rather like cowslips, indeed the former is often referred to as the Himalayan Cowslip, but unlike our native kind grows to a height of some three or four feet. *Primula sikkimensis* is almost identical but considerably smaller with soft yellow flowers that are deliciously fragrant. *Primula microdonta alpicola* and its variety *violacea* are of similar habit with drooping blooms in pendant clusters, but are additionally dusted liberally with white or yellowish meal. The species is soft yellow, while its variety as one might expect, is deep violet-mauve.

Primula waltonii has clustered flowers of deep port wine, and *P. helodoxa* stout stems bearing whorls of rich yellow blooms. Finally just a mention of what is probably the most bizarre and remarkable member of the genus *P. viali*. Although often not long-lived, this striking character brightens up a shady corner with flower spikes of red and lilac in shape and contrast like those of a red hot poker or Kniphofia, but of course much smaller.

Numerous other species and varieties exist, but those mentioned are the ones most readily available. All as intimated earlier are easily grown in moist conditions and provide the gardener with a range of shapes, sizes and colours to suit all situations. All can be propagated by seed sown immediately it ripens or by spring division of the crowns.

RHEUM Rhubarb

There are a number of decorative rhubarbs that are of value in the marsh garden. In the smaller garden they can emulate *Gunnera manicata* with their broad spreading leaves, but they cannot replace it. *Rheum palmatum* is the most widely grown species with broad spreading foliage and spikes of creamy-white blooms some five or six feet high. A variety called *tanguticum* has much divided foliage and crimson or deep rose flowers, while the cultivar 'Bowles Crimson' or 'Atropurpureum' as it is known in some quarters, has foliage suffused with deep purplish-red.

Several other species are cultivated, but only *R. nobile*, a curious variety with four foot high spires of fawn coloured bracts is at home in the bog garden, the others are much happier in the wild garden or shrubbery. Propagation by seed, division or root cuttings.

SYMPLOCARPUS   Skunk Cabbage

Symplocarpus foetidus is a curiosity rather than a plant of beauty, producing quaintly hooded arum-like flowers of purple and green in the early spring long before its cabbagey leaves have appeared. The flowers which are four or five inches high are slightly malodorous but extremely offensive if bruised or crushed. Propagation by division.

TROLLIUS   Globe Flower

The Trollius family is a group of striking buttercup-like perennials with attractive incurved heads of yellow or orange. *Trollius europaeus*, a soft yellow species and the bold *T. asiaticus* are the parents of most garden hybrids and, although valuable additions to the bog garden themselves, the cultivar forms such as 'Orange Princess', 'Canary Bird', and the deep orange 'Fire Globe', are much improved. Where space is limited the diminutive yellow flowered *T. pumilus* and more particularly the improved 'Wargrave Variety', coupled with the even tinier *T. yunnanensis* ensure that the most modest bog garden can accommodate a clump or two of these handsome plants. Propagation of the species by seed or division and the cultivars by division.

(Right) *Typha latifolia*, the Reedmace, often erroneously called the Bulrush.

(Below) *Stratiotes aloides*, the Water Soldier.

(Left) *Eichornia crassipes*, the Water Hyacinth.

(Below) *Limnocharis humboldtii*, the Water Poppy; *Azolla caroliniana*, Fairy Moss.

(6)

Plants for the Heated or Indoor Pool

Stocking an indoor, or outdoor pool of the heated variety, follows along the same lines as the straight-forward garden pond except that the choice of planting material is much greater. Unfortunately, although the tropical species of aquatic plants outnumber by at least two to one those from temperate climes, their appearance in nurserymen's lists is most conspicuous by its absence. I have therefore deemed it wise to restrict my selection of suitable subjects to those that are commercially available, even if sometimes difficult to locate, and those that are of modest enough proportions for the ordinary gardener to be able to accommodate.

TROPICAL WATERLILIES
There are several different methods of growing tropical waterlilies, but in this country they are generally confined to tub and heated pool culture, although with a little attention they will thrive outside in the ordinary garden pond.

Preliminary Potting
Usually on arrival from the nurseries in early spring, the plants are in a dormant state and appear as rather coarse, rounded, chestnut-like tubers. They should be inspected immediately for soft areas on the surface and, when soaked in water for an hour or so, should become heavy and sink; those that do not are likely to be of little use, remaining dormant for several months, or just rotting away and leaving an empty, scaly skin behind.

Having satisfied oneself that the tubers are absolutely sound, pot them individually in three-inch pots in the same compost as recommended for their hardy counterparts (see p. 62). Stand the pots in an aquarium or shallow tray of water, in a temperature of between 65° and 70°F and place in a position of full sunlight. After a few days, juvenile underwater foliage will appear, followed a week or so later by the rounded, floating, adult leaves. At this stage the plants can be transferred to their permanent quarters. If one or two tubers have shown no signs of sprouting by this time, remove them from their pots, re-pot in coarse washed sand and return them to the tray or aquarium. For some inexplicable reason, this is often enough to jog them into active growth, after which they can be potted once again in ordinary compost.

Barrels

When tubs are used for planting, these often prove to be second-hand barrels which have been sawn in half and made watertight. Whilst not wishing to condemn a gardener his enterprise, I do think that a few words regarding the suitability of barrels that have previously contained substances other than water, are in order at this point. Old wine or vinegar casks are admirable, as are beer barrels, but those which have contained fats, oils, tar or wood preservative should be avoided, as any residue that remains will pollute the water, forming an unsightly scum on the surface. Before attempting to plant anything in a newly-made tub, give it a good scrubbing inside with clear water and then thoroughly rinse it out. On no account use detergent for cleaning, as it is difficult to be sure when all traces have been removed. Tubs that have been used before, often become coated on the inside with a thick growth of slime and algae, and where it is felt that water alone is an insufficient cleansing agent, then the addition of enough potassium permanganate to turn the water a violet colour will usually have the desired effect.

Planting

By the time the waterlilies are ready to plant in their permanent home, it is getting towards the end of April or beginning of May. They should be planted with just their crowns protruding above the soil, only one plant being allowed to each tub and even then some of the larger varieties will be cramped. Water is added gradually as the plants grow and should be kept at a temperature of between 55° and 60°F. The advantage with tub culture is that this can easily be done by the introduction of an ordinary aquarium heater, which rapidly warms up small bodies of water and, in conjunction with a thermostat to control the temperature, proves to be a particularly cheap and efficient means of heating.

Planting in the pool is almost identical, except that the plants should remain potted for a greater length of time; being moved to successively larger pots until in full growth sometime during June. The main reason for doing this is to give them a good start when plunged into deep water, for small sprouted tubers often have a tremendous struggle to become established under such conditions, whereas a large plant removed from its pot with root-ball intact, will hardly realise it has been transplanted and will grow away vigorously.

Winter Storage
Nothing much need be done with the plants during the summer months, except for the periodic check for pests and the occasional topping up of the tubs with fresh water. But as soon as September approaches and the nights start drawing in, the water should if possible be gradually lowered and the mud allowed to dry out, or in the garden pool the baskets removed and dried out slowly. This causes the top growth to die away and ripens the tubers, which are then lifted for storing. Damp sand is the best medium to store them in and should be contained in a vermin-proof box of some kind and kept in a frost-proof place. I use an old cake tin, in which I lay the tubers out in rows sandwiched between inch-deep layers of sand. They keep very well for the winter months without any attention and should not be interfered with until planting time the following spring. Many growers do not even bother with storing, but treat the plants as annuals and purchase fresh stock each year. Indeed, this has much to commend it for young tubers are often more active and grow into far superior plants than the older woody ones.

Varieties

As with the various hardy species and hybrids, the list of popular and suitable tropical varieties has been compiled in alphabetical rather than botanical order and the hybrids of uncertain origin divided into two groups—nocturnal and day blooming.

TROPICAL SPECIES AND THEIR VARIETIES

Nymphaea amazonum : Large sweetly scented creamy-white flowers about three inches across with thick velvety petals. The handsome heart-shaped or oval floating leaves have reddish-brown undersides. Nocturnal. (1½-2 ft.)

N. capensis: (syn. *N. emirensis*) Cape Blue Waterlily. A popular and very beautiful variety with fragrant bright blue flowers borne amidst dark-green foliage that is liberally splashed with purplish-blue. (1½-2 ft.)

N. coerulea: Blue Nile Lotus. Beautiful sky-blue flowers up to nine inches across with black spotted sepals are held on slender stems above dark-green oval foliage. A white variety *N.c.var. albiflora* is the same but devoid of the black markings on the sepals. (1½-2 ft.)

N. colorata: A handsome plant with small purple or lilac flowers with very broad petals and masses of rounded dark-green foliage. (1½-2 ft.)

N. flava: (syn. *N. mexicana*) An almost hardy species which reproduces by means of suckers. Its tiny canary-yellow flowers are carried amongst olive-green foliage that is heavily blotched with purple. (1 ft.)

N. gigantea: Immense sky blue flowers with golden stamens that attain a diameter of quite fifteen inches under favourable conditions. A veritable giant. (1½-3 ft.)

N. lotus: White Nile Lotus. A handsome species with deliciously scented pure white flowers up to eight inches across and abundant peltate floating leaves. The seeds and tubers are edible and used as food in some parts of Africa. Nocturnal. (1½-2½ ft.)

N. stellata: Star-shaped blooms of blue or occasionally white. The true blue and most desirable type has golden stamens, black spotted sepals and narrowly pointed petals which lighten towards the base. Its foliage is large, of a roughly orbicular or elliptical shape and with violet undersides. A most desirable hybrid called 'Berlin' is becoming quite popular and has very large and fine sky blue flowers. (1½-2½ ft.)

DAY BLOOMING HYBRIDS

AFRICAN GOLD: Small intense yellow blooms and smallish rounded pale green leaves. (1-1½ ft.)

AMERICAN BEAUTY: Immense pale plum-coloured flowers with fluorescent yellow centres are borne amidst large orbicular green leaves with wavy margins and bright red undersides. (2-3 ft.)

AUGUST KOCH: An excellent cut-flower variety with mid-blue flowers held high above the water. Strongly viviparous. (1½-2½ ft.)

BLUE BEAUTY: An old and very fine variety derived from a union between *N. coerulea* and *N. capensis var. zanzibariensis.* Deep blue flowers with a central golden disc from which the yellow stamens with violet anthers are produced. (2½-3½ ft.)

GENERAL PERSHING: Huge pink flowers which remain continually open are borne at least a foot above water level. The young buds are green with conspicuous purple stripes and the leaves are green streaked with red. (2½-3½ ft.)

JUDGE HITCHCOCK: Broad cup-shaped blooms of purplish-blue intensifying to violet towards the tips of the petals. Small dark green leaves flecked with brown and deep purple beneath. (1½-2½ ft.)

MIDNIGHT: A curious variety with small rich purple flowers consisting of several large broad outer petals and a cluster of small modified petals around the tiny golden centre. Small dark green leaves flecked with brown and deep purple beneath. (1½-2½ ft.)

MRS. GEORGE H. PRING: A beautiful variety with large white star-like blooms and fresh green leaves daubed with reddish-brown. (1-3 ft.)

PANAMA PACIFIC: A blue flowered variety which changes to rich purple with age. Strongly viviparous. (1½-2½ ft.)

NIGHT BLOOMING HYBRIDS
The night blooming varieties are generally stronger, more robust, plants than their day flowering counterparts. Most are derived from crosses between *N. lotus*, *N. rubra* and *N. amazonum* and various forms of those species.

B.C. BERRY: Large shallow flowers of amaranth-purple shading lighter towards the centre. The leaves are of a medium size with a faint purplish mottling and heavily indented margins. (1½-2½ ft.)

EMILY GRANT HUTCHINGS: Large pinkish-red cup-shaped blooms with deep amaranth stamens which become rich mahogany with age. The sepals and foliage have a distinctive bronzed-crimson overlay. (1½-2½ ft.)

JAMES GURNEY: Fragrant flowers of deep rose-pink which may be up to ten inches across with elongated petals surrounding a central boss of orange stamens, are held high above the water. The large orbicular leaves with fluted margins are coppery-green above and purple beneath. (2½-3½ ft.)

MISSOURI: Immense flowers up to fifteen inches across and of the purest white are held high above the water on thick succulent flower stems. The petals are broad and surround a central boss of erect golden stamens. The dark green leaves with indented margins are strikingly mottled with purple and brown. (2½-3½ ft.)

SOME GOOD TENDER AQUATICS

Apart from the very obvious beauty displayed by the tropical Nymphaeas, it should be remembered that there are many other very fine aquatics which are worthy of cultivation in an indoor pool. A number of these, especially of the submerged oxygenating kinds are described as aquarium plants so a repetition of their appearance and needs under this heading is unnecessary. Those that follow are basically marginal and floating plants, but each is particularly valuable to the indoor gardener.

EICHORNIA Water Hyacinth

The Water Hyacinth, *Eichornia crassipes*, is a tropical floating plant of exceeding beauty. It consists basically of a cluster of shiny dark-green leaves with grossly inflated bases which are filled with air and resemble small balloons. The flowers which are produced during late summer are carried on a short stiff spike and resemble a beautiful blue and lilac orchid. Although not hardy, the Water Hyacinth can be relied upon to grow well in an outdoor pool, producing several young plants on thick fleshy runners during the course of the season.

Plants should be floated on the pool when all danger of frost has passed, usually during early June and returned to the greenhouse about mid-September. Young plants should be chosen as over-wintering stock and will keep quite well if allowed to root in a pan of wet mud. However, in common with many pool-owners, I feel the time and trouble spent in trying to over-winter young specimens is not commensurate with the return and prefer to invest twenty-five or thirty pence in a new plant each spring and treat it as an annual.

In the heated indoor pool, Eichornia grows at a tremendous rate, producing surprisingly tall plants and an abundance of bloom. Unfortunately these large plants are unsuitable for over-wintering, and little side-shoots or runners should once again be removed and rooted in wet mud.

HYDROCLEYS Water Poppy

The Water Poppy, *Hydrocleys commersonii (syn. Linmocharis*

humboldtii, L. commersonii) is an exceptionally fine aquatic for six or eight inches of water. It produces oval fleshy leaves of deep pea-green colour and handsome golden three petalled flowers just above the surface of the water. Although hardy in very sheltered districts, it is always advisable to take a few cuttings or rooted pieces inside before there is any likelihood of a frost, so that the stock can be perpetuated or increased if necessary the following spring. In the indoor pool it can sometimes be invasive, but is easily contained by regular cutting back.

NELUMBIUM   Sacred Lotus

Nelumbiums are half-hardy aquatics with handsome, glaucous, plate-like leaves held above the water on centrally placed petioles which may be anything up to eight feet high. The upper surfaces of the leaves are coated with a thin waxy substance, so that when a drop of water falls onto them it runs about like quick-silver. The waterlily-like flowers are borne on long, slender stems which extend to just above the leaves and are followed by curious seed heads which resemble the roses of small watering cans.

Cultivation is the same as that advocated for tropical waterlilies. The whitish, banana-like rootstocks come to hand during March and should be planted in round tubs, in a heavy loam compost enriched with a handful of coarse bonemeal. Plant horizontally, about an inch beneath the soil and then add two or three inches of water. As the young foliage emerges gradually raise the level of the water until it is about nine inches deep. Routine summer care is confined to watching for aphids and supporting any foliage that becomes top heavy. As autumn approaches, slowly drain the water off so that the foliage dies down. Then the roots may be lifted, washed and stored in boxes of damp sand for the winter.

Propagation is usually effected by breaking off the tubers at the points where they narrow, ensuring that each portion has a terminal shoot, and then planting in the normal manner. The species, however, are also readily propagated by seeds which are sown singly in pots of heavy loam and placed in a tank of water which is kept at a temperature of 75°-80°F. The juvenile leaves will float on the surface, but as the plants grow stronger they are thrust up above it in typical fashion. Pot on as and when necessary in the same heavy loam, but with a sprinkling of coarse bonemeal added. After about two years they will have reached maturity and can then be expected to run into flower.

The Species and their Varieties

N. luteum: *(syn. Nelumbo lutea, N. pentapetala)*. American Lotus, Duck Acorn, Water Chinkapin. Large leaves two feet across are borne on stems up to three feet high. The flowers are up to eight inches across and of a uniform shade of pale sulphur yellow. Does not flower freely until well established.

Var. flavescens: Smaller flowers than the preceding, but the same shade of pale yellow. There is a conspicuous red spot at the base of each petal and in the centre of each leaf.

N. speciosum: *(syn. Nelumbo nucifera. Nelumbium indica)*. Immense blooms, up to twelve inches across, change from vivid rose to flesh pink with age. Large rounded leaves on petioles up to six or even eight feet high.

Var. album: The Magnolia Lotus. A pure white form of the type.

Var. album grandiflorum: *(syn. Nelumbo, alba var. floribunda)*. Immense, fragrant, ivory goblets in excess of a foot across with a central boss of golden stamens, are held high above large pea-green leaves.

Var. album plenum: *(syn. Shiroman)*. A Japanese selection with large fragrant, double, creamy-white flowers intensifying to pure white with age.

Var. album striatum: *(syn. Empress)*. Pure white blooms tipped and streaked with crimson. Very fragrant.

Var. album virens: Rounded, double white flowers flushed and stained with green when young, but clearing to pure white with age.

Var. gigantea: Enormous purplish-rose flowers amidst immense pea-green leaves with silvery reverses.

Var. roseum: *(syn. Dawn).* Large flowers of delicate pale pink.

Var. roseum plenum: *(syn. Double Dawn).* The much deeper coloured double form.

Hybrids

GROSSHERZOG ERNST LUDWIG : A hybrid between *N. luteum var. flavescens* and *N. × Osiris.* The exotic blooms, like rosy-red brandy glasses, have golden stamens and conspicuous green ovaries, and are borne above handsome sea-green foliage.

JAPONICA ROSEA : Large double flowers flushed and overlaid with rose. Glaucous foliage.

KERMESINA : A very fine double red variety of Japanese origin.

KINSHIREN : Medium sized white blooms flushed with soft rose-pink.

LILYPONS : Large salmon-pink cup-shaped flowers.

MADAME PAUFIGUE : White flowers flushed with carmine.

OSIRIS : Probably the most popular Nelumbium hybrid. Huge globular rose-pink blooms and bluish-green foliage.

PEKINENSIS RUBRA : Intense, very fragrant, dark crimson flowers with a thick velvety texture to the petals.

PEKINENSIS RUBRA PLENA : A much less floriferous, yet most striking double form.

PULCHRA : Lavender-rose blooms streaked and lined with red.

PYGMAEA ALBA : A completely miniature form with leaves no more than a foot high or six inches across and pure white flowers seldom in excess of four inches in diameter.

PYGMAEA ALBA PLENA : A double-flowered form of the preceding.

PYGMAEA ROSEA : Tiny single flowers of intense rose-pink.

VIOLACEA : Deep plum-red flowers lightly streaked and veined with white. Tends to be a shy bloomer until well established.

THALIA

A handsome marginal plant somewhat reminiscent of a Canna is probably the best way to describe *Thalia dealbata*. With tall greyish leaves some five feet high, and arching sprays of small purplish flowers it is a distinctive and unusual plant for the pool. Although a North American native it cannot be trusted to be hardy and is therefore best grown in baskets or pots which can easily be moved indoors for the winter months. When grown permanently indoors it tends to become lanky and untidy looking, even if given adequate ventilation. The secret with Thalia would appear to be to grow it cool but not allow it to be frosted. Propagation is by division of the emerging shoots in early spring.

ZANTEDESCHIA   Arum Lily

The common Florist Arum, *Zantedeschia aethiopica* is a similar proposition to the plant Thalia previously described and best treated as an aquatic bedding plant. There are many varieties in commerce, but only the familiar white species is suitable for pool conditions. Growing to a height of some three feet or so, it produces handsome shiny dark-green foliage and waxy white blooms so beloved of the floral arranger. Some gardeners claim to be able to over-winter arums successfully by growing them in deep water—up to fifteen inches—and for those in milder districts, I would think this worth considering.

(7)

Aquarium Plants

Most of the plants advocated as submerged oxygenating plants suitable for pond culture are eminently suited to aquarium life. With a few exceptions, the floating plants used in the pool are also useful while small. Tiny Water Soldiers *Stratiotes aloides* and the frogbit *Hydrocharis morsus-ranae* will soon outgrow their allocated space, although they are useful as temporary inhabitants. Several species of submerged plants often grow better in a well lighted aquarium than in their natural environment, particularly those such as Callitriche and Myriophyllum, although the temperature must remain relatively cool. Fontinalis and Ceratophyllum are useful spawning plants and particularly valuable as they do not object to subdued light, but once again they dislike excessively warm water. Several other plants that are capable of growing quite happily in cold water aquaria, although usually classed as tropical plants are included in the following survey, but their adaptability is duly noted in the description.

SUBMERGED PLANTS

ACORUS Sweet Flag
See description of diminutive species under marginal plants (page 82).

ANUBIAS Water Aspidistra
The very distinctive *Anubias lanceolata*, as its common name belies, is like an underwater version of the old Victorian Aspidistra. It has thick shiny green leaves borne on short stout stems that arise from a tuber-like rhizome and, like its terrestrial replica, can be relied upon to grow well in shade. A comparatively recent—mid

1930s—introduction from the old French Guinea, this plant is now widely commercialised and available from most aquarists' shops. In fact, if a friend has a plant, it is an easy matter, with his co-operation, to divide the tuber into several pieces each of which will rapidly form new plants.

APONOGETON   Water Hawthorn

The most popular and best known member of this genus is the hardy *A. distachyus* described earlier; however, there are a number of tropical species somewhat less vigorous, but equally attractive in their way. *Aponogeton crispum* from Ceylon is probably the easiest to come by as dormant tubers of this variety are imported by growers into this country by the thousand. They are started into growth in a warm tank and sold some two weeks later with a tuft of leaves on the top. It is always advisable to buy plants which have been started rather than dry tubers which are often sold at about half the price, as inducing the latter to break dormancy is a somewhat unpredictable business. When happily settled in an aquarium, it is a most attractive species with almost translucent leaves on narrow stems, and forked spikes of somewhat feathery flowers just above water level.

The Madagascan *A. ulvaceous* is of similar character with broader leaves with attractively waved and crimpled edges. Like *A. crispum* it is propagated from seed or division of the tuber.

Although not really a plant to consider for the average aquarium, so individual are its needs, *A. fenestralis* the universally-known Madagascar Lace Plant, must find a place here. It is a plant of exceeding beauty, with incomplete leaves some eighteen inches long by four inches wide which consist entirely of a network of nerves and veins. The leaves are devoid of any vestige of what one might term lamina, and have evolved in such a manner by existing in dark murky waters at great depths. Thus it follows that these are difficult conditions to provide in an aquarium. Indeed, the best plants of this species are grown in barrels so that direct light in a horizontal plane is eliminated. They also require moving water which is of a low pH if they are to thrive.

Some years ago when I was a student at the Cambridge Botanic

Garden *A. fenestralis* was grown with considerable success in a sink-like tank in a warm greenhouse. Above the tank was a jerry can with a tap which was periodically refilled with distilled water. The tap was left to drip and the falling water landed in a funnel full of saturated sedge peat and from there trickled slowly into the tank. Although it grew satisfactorily it never to my knowledge set seed with which to attempt propagation.

CABOMBA Fanworts

All species of Cabomba make excellent aquarium plants. They are, however, marred by the fact that they soon become leggy and are beloved of many tropical fish which take a great delight in denuding them completely. *Cabomba caroliniana* is the one usually encountered in pet stores and has slender stems bearing bright green coarsely cut fan-shaped leaves. A variety with rose-pink foliage *C. caroliniana* 'Rosaefolia' is very pleasing to the eye but difficult to come by. *Cabomba aquatica* is another species sometimes offered and differs principally from its cousins in that it has two types of foliage; kidney-shaped floating leaves and coarse cut submerged foliage. All kinds are easily propagated from cuttings.

CRYPTOCORYNE Water Trumpet

Unbelievably at first glance members of the Arum family, these charming little fellows are beloved by aquarists because of their variety and relatively slow rate of growth. The genus contains some forty or so species of which only about a dozen are ever located in commerce. In fact in Britain little study has been made of these plants, whereas in both Holland and Germany they are grown by the thousand for export and considerable work has been undertaken to study their mode of growth.

Cryptocoryne cordata is the species most generally cultivated and has yellowish-green cordate leaves borne on green or pale reddish stems. The undersides of the foliage is a striking purple and looks most exotic when growing in congested clumps of a dozen or more leaves at a time in the centre of a well-stocked aquarium. For the small tank or the foreground of a larger type there is the very easy going dwarf variety *C. beckettii*. This has narrow leaves of a bright green hue that seldom exceed four inches in length. Apart from these two there are three further kinds not infrequently encountered: *C. ciliata* with foot high narrow stalked leaves of a mid-green shade and thick somewhat fleshy texture; *C. griffithii* with broad cordate foliage of rich satiny green and the comparatively small *C. willisii* with its compact crinkly edged foliage. All kinds can be propagated by careful division.

ECHINODORUS

One of the finest aquarium centre pieces is to be found within this genus and that is the mighty Amazon Sword Plant, *E. intermedius*. In ample light and a temperature of at least 75°F it flourishes, producing bold sword-like leaves on stout stems. An outstanding plant for the spacious aquarium.

The closely allied *E. radicans* is not quite as spectacular but is a superior oxygenator by all accounts. Under the same conditions as its illustrious cousin it bears very fine lanceolate leaves quite six inches long at right angles to the stem. In shallow water it produces aerial foliage of an unsightly nature, so is best kept in a tank with at least twelve inches of water. Both species respond to very careful division of the crowns which are best started into growth in shallow water, or by seeds sown directly on to trays of wet mud.

EGERIA

Under this name is the plant formerly known to the trade as *Elodea densa*. A native of South America, notably the Argentine, this robust little chap is equally at home in cold or tropical waters. It is of similar habit to *Elodea crispa* (now *Lagarosiphon major*), but with slightly smaller deep green foliage. The Brazilian form which goes under the name *E. densa var. longifolia* would seem to be a geographical variation. With longer leaves and rapid growth, this particular form is a must for the tropical aquarium. Both forms are easily propagated from short stem cuttings bunched together with a lead weight and then pushed into the gravel.

HETERANTHERA

Of the fifteen or so species of Heteranthera, only two are at all common, or indeed really suited to aquarium life. These are the Water Stargrass *H. graminea*, and *H. zosteraefolia*. Both look super-

ficially like *Egeria densa*, producing long dense growths that are
ideal for spawning, but unlike Egeria the leaves instead of growing
in whorls, branch alternately from both sides of the stem. In good
light flowering is abundant, the tiny floating blooms of *H. graminea*
being pale yellow in colour while those of *H. zosteraefolia* are soft
blue. Propagation is by division.

HYDRILLA

The very useful and easy going *H. verticillata* is another plant of
similar growth to *Egeria densa*. In strong light growth is prolific,
dense whorls of olive-green foliage being borne at intervals up
short stout stems. To do well it requires plenty of heat and when
this is provided it more than amply repays its keep from both an
aesthetic and oxygenating point of view. Easily propagated from
cuttings bunched together with a piece of lead and pushed well into
the gravel.

HYDROTRIDA

The familiar *H. caroliniana*, which is more often known as *Bacopa
amplexicaulis* or *Herpestris amplexicaulis*, is a popular inhabitant
of the tropical tank. It is surprisingly a somewhat hairy plant with
thick oval leaves on strong stout stems. In shallow water masses
of rich blue axillary flowers are produced, but under ordinary
aquarium conditions these are unfortunately seldom forthcoming
and the rate of vegetative growth is also reduced. Propagation is
from cuttings.

HYGROPHILA

Although a comparatively recent introduction to the aquarium
scene, this Ludwigia-like plant should find its way into any sizeable
set-up. The species grown is *H. polysperma*, a broad leafed plant
with bright green foliage and purplish stems. It is seen at its best
when massed amongst rock-work, the occasional stem spilling out
and rooting at the node in the gravel below. However, for those of
tidier mind a bushy form can be developed by continually pinching
back the shoots. Being a native of India it obviously requires plenty
of heat and good light if it is to do well.

LIMNOPHILA

Sometimes sold by dealers erroneously under the name of Ambulia, *Limnophila sessiliflora* in outward appearance seems closely allied to Cabomba. Here, however, the similarities end for Limnophila is a painfully slow grower, its vivid emerald green foliage being produced over a considerable period of time on slender branching stems. *Limnophila heterophylla* is almost identical but favoured by some aquarists. Propagation is by cuttings inserted in a sandy medium in a very warm tank.

LUDWIGIA   False Loosestrife

Ludwigia palustris has already been described in the section dealing with marginal plants and this is really what the Ludwigias are. However, several species adapt well to a submerged existence and are among the finest broad-leafed aquatics for the aquarium. *Ludwigia mulertii* is undoubtably the best known, producing handsome lanceolate leaves of bronzy-green with crimson-purple undersides. Tropical conditions bring out the best in this plant, but it will grow satisfactorily under coldwater conditions. *Ludwigia microcarpa* though is strictly a tropical plant of slightly smaller stature than its brother, but with striking reddish-bronze rounded leaves. Propagation is by cuttings.

MARSILEA   Foil Plant, Water Clover

Although not of much value as oxygenating plants, many aquarists introduce the various species of Marsilea into their tanks for the sake of variety. To the layman they appear as four-leaf clovers on extended leaf stalks which reach upward and support their rounded leaves on the surface of the water. In actual fact they are really ferns, although their appearance does not reveal their affinity and they are consequently totally bereft of the flowers that one feels they ought to be able to produce. This unfortunate state of affairs is corrected somewhat by the unusual character of the unfurling leaves beneath the water, for on breaking open they appear as tin foil, the air from within being trapped on the hirsute surface of the leaves. This persists for maybe forty-eight hours until the minute bubbles have dispersed.

Several species are offered by aquatics dealers but all look very similar. *M. quadrifolia* is the commonest kind, but *M. fimbriata* and *M. drummondii* are also often located. All are almost hardy and make admirable subjects for the coldwater aquarium and all can be readily propagated by division of the extensive creeping rootstock.

MYRIOPHYLLUM   Milfoil

All the species described as suitable for pool culture are excellent for the coldwater aquarium, but generally too vigorous to do much good in a tropical environment. *Myriophyllum hippuroides* and *M. scabratum* from the warmer parts of America are ideal. The former has bright green feathery foliage of typical milfoil form, while his companion is clothed in particularly beautiful leaves of a reddish-bronze colour and crowned at odd times with small spikes of purple flowers. As with their hardy counterparts these two delightful fellows make an excellent spawning medium, the hair-like leaflets providing young fry with plenty of cover. Propagation of the plants, which should be undertaken fairly frequently if a straggly appearance is to be avoided, is by cuttings of fresh vigorous growth.

NAJAS   Naiads

An Elodea-like annual of particular value in the coldwater aquarium. Its crinkly translucent leaves are borne in pairs and are of a delightful shade of emerald green. Inconspicuous axillary flowers are often produced and seed freely, although the best method of propagation is by cuttings.

NITELLA

Rootless plants closely allied to Chara and similarly of great value to the fish breeder as a spawning ground. The popular *N. gracilis* is a dense somewhat wiry plant of deep bluish-green colour and in common with other stonewort-like plants is a first class oxygenator. It is really a coldwater plant but adapts quite readily to higher temperatures. Propagation is simply by dividing and redistributing the tangled mass of foliage.

SAGITTARIA   Arrowhead

Most people are familiar with this genus as the one that provides

us with attractive white flowered marginal plants that add colour
to the pool side during the shortening days of late summer. However, to the aquarist they are rushy underwater plants of immense
value. Both *S. lorata* and the tiny *S. subulata* are excellent oxygenators and produce upright clumps of dark-green spring onion-like
plants. These are crowned during summer with floating oval or
arrow-shaped foliage and tiny white flowers. Like their semi-
terrestrial relatives they produce tiny turions and these, together
with an onion-like shoot, can be detached and replanted when more
plants are needed. Coldwater conditions suit them fine, but they
do not object to tropical temperatures and when planted in such,
carpet the aquarium very rapidly.

VALLISNERIA Tape Grass
Of all aquarium plants, the common *V. spiralis* is probably best
known. It is a broad tape-like but grassy foliage plant with tiny
insignificant whitish flowers. It is most adaptable as to conditions,
thriving in both cold and tropical waters thus being probably the
best submerged plant the novice can acquire in his early ventures.
Indeed, in my opinion, one cannot do better than select a plant or
two of the handsome cultivated form known as 'Torta'. This is
identical to the species but has leaves that are twisted evenly in a
corkscrew fashion.

For really large aquaria the giant *V. gigantea* is excellent and can
also be used to considerable effect in 'framing' the scene in a
smaller tank. A particularly fine form is *V. gigantea* 'Rubrifolia'
with bronze and crimson foliage, a complete contrast to the baby
of the genus *V. minor*. This has tiny green almost transparent
foliage and is excellent for the small coldwater aquarium. Propagation is by division of the plantlets.

FLOATING PLANTS

In addition to those recommended for outdoor pool culture, which
can in most cases be successfully grown in a coldwater aquarium,
and those that have been recommended for the indoor pool which
obviously are quite at home in the tropical tank, there are several
that are aquarium plants pure and simple.

CERATOPTERIS   Floating Fern

Two species of these exceedingly handsome Pteridophytes are commonly grown by aquarists, but only *C. pteridoides* is a truly floating plant, the more vigorous *C. thalictroides* tending to root in the gravel and grow submerged. Both have attractive green heart-shaped or lanceolate leaves with wavy edges which are entirely barren, but which surround the upward growing clump of fertile fronds and give the entire plant the appearance of a rosette. Propagation is by young plantlets which appear in profusion on the edges of mature leaves.

RICCIA   Crystalwort

This is a very popular spawn plant which is known by many as Crystalwort. Both *R. fluitans* and *R. natans* are vigorous oxygenators which form masses of starry foliage at the water's surface and collect in thick mats several inches deep. Propagation by division.

SALVINIA

Although there are supposedly three species of Salvinia in cultivation, *S. auriculata*, *S. natans* and *S. braziliensis*, they are so close to one another that I would doubt if any but the most ardent botanist could distinguish between them. Indeed, even he would in all probability be frustrated because all three species are generally sold mixed together under the collective name Salvinia. All are of a diminutive character with oval velvety foliage which clings to a dark wiry stem. Like many other small floating plants such as duckweeds and Fairy Moss, Salvinia can get out of hand and then has to be netted off vigorously and disposed of. However, this seems to be related directly to the acidity of the water and often plants growing in conditions of high pH fail to grow or reproduce satisfactorily and often die. Propagation is by division and redistribution.

(8)

Pests and Diseases

As may be expected aquatic plants, in common with their terrestrial counterparts, suffer to some extent from pests and diseases. Fortunately those that are specific to these plants are few and far between, but those that do attack can be extremely difficult to eradicate, especially when there are fish present, for the slightest trace of insecticide or fungicide in a pool usually proves fatal to the inmates—fish and snails alike.

PESTS

Waterlily Aphis
Although several species of aphis attack waterlilies, *Rhopalosiphum nymphaea* is by far the most troublesome. In warm humid weather it breeds at a prodigious rate, absolutely smothering the plants and causing widespread disfigurement of both flowers and foliage. It is usually noticed on waterlily foliage, but will also attack other succulent aquatics such as Butomus and Sagittaria.

Eggs from the late summer brood of adults are laid on the boughs of plum and cherry trees during early autumn for over-wintering. These hatch the following spring and the winged female adults fly to the plants. Here they reproduce asexually, giving birth to live wingless females which continue the process every few days. As autumn approaches once again, winged males and females are produced which unite sexually and then fly to plum and cherry trees to deposit their eggs.

During the summer months a contact wash, such as pyrethrum or nicotine soap, can be applied to the foliage providing, of course, that there are no fish present. Otherwise the only satisfactory remedy is to spray the entire plant forcibly with a jet of clear water in order to dislodge the pests and give the fish a chance to get at them. In winter, the spraying of any nearby plum or cherry trees with DNOC Tar Oil winter wash will help considerably to reduce the aphid population the following spring.

Waterlily Beetle

The Waterlily Beetle, *Galerucella nymphaea*, is an important and extremely troublesome pest which fortunately is usually only of local occurrence. The small dark brown beetles and shiny black larvae will usually be found on lily 'pads', where the latter strips the epidermal layer of tissue from both flower and foliage, leaving the tattered slimy remains to decay.

The adult beetle hibernates during the winter in pond-side vegetation and migrates to waterlilies during early June. Here it deposits its eggs in clusters on the leaf surfaces. After about a week they hatch out into curious black larvae with distinctive yellow bellies. These feed on the 'pads' until pupation takes place, either on the foliage or surrounding aquatic plants. Under favourable conditions there may be three, or even four, broods in a season.

When fish are present, nothing except forcible spraying with clear water can be recommended, although removing the tops of marginal plants during early autumn will do much to prevent the adults from hibernating in the immediate vicinity and will perhaps dissuade them from launching another attack the following year. Where there are no fish, and no danger of pets drinking the water, then spraying with malathion is an effective cure.

Beautiful China Mark Moth

The Beautiful China Mark Moth, *Nymphula stagnata*, is a very similar species to the next discussed, except that the caterpillars burrow into the stems of aquatic plants in the early stages of their life. In due course they hibernate there, but later emerge to make leaf cases and subsequently their white silky cocoons. As yet there is no control other than hand picking.

Brown China Mark Moth

The larvae of this comparatively insignificant brown and orange moth is probably the greatest menace the pond-owner will have to contend with, for not only does it cut and shred the foliage of aquatic plants, but also makes a shelter for itself, prior to pupation, by sticking down two pieces of leaf in which it weaves a greyish silky cocoon. The damage to a plant can well be imagined; chewed and distorted leaves crumbling towards the edges, surrounded by floating pieces of rapidly decaying foliage.

Eggs of the Brown China Mark Moth, *Nymphula nympheata*, are laid during late summer in neat rows along the undersides of floating leaves and hatch out after about a fortnight. The tiny caterpillars burrow into the undersides of the juicy foliage and later make small oval cases out of these leaves. They continue to feed and grow until the winter, when most of their food supply is exhausted. Nobody really knows what happens to them during the cold winter months, but they re-appear the ensuing spring to cause more damage and weave the cocoons already described, prior to pupation.

Small infestations can be hand picked, but do not neglect to remove pieces of leaf that may be floating around in the water, for these may also have cocoons attached. When damage is widespread, I find it better to remove all the floating leaves and destroy them, thereby giving the plant a completely fresh start. As yet, no satisfactory chemical control has been devised.

Bobitis Nelumbialis
A curious insect pest with no common name, which is seldom encountered in this country and is specific to the Lotus or Nelumbium species. It is recognisable as a small grub which has rolled and gummed itself between the edges of young leaves, which it then feeds on in comparative safety. Hand picking is the only control, although nicotine spraying is advocated in the absence of fish.

Caddis Flies
Most of the one hundred and eighty-five British species of caddis fly have larvae which feed to some extent on the foliage of aquatic plants. Many of them are totally aquatic in their larval stage and

swim with little shelters made of sticks, sand, shells and pieces of plant surrounding them. All are members of the order Trichoptera and the species *Halesus radiatus* and *Limnephilus marmoratus* are especially common.

The flies visit the pool in the cool of the evening, depositing up to a hundred eggs at a time in a mass of jelly which swells up immediately it touches the water. Often this is hooked around submerged foliage in a long cylindrical string, or attached to some marginal plant which will allow it to trail in the water. After about ten days the larvae hatch out, immediately starting to spin their silken cases and collecting material with which to construct their shelters. At this stage they feed on water plants, devouring leaves, stems, flowers and roots with equal indifference. Later they pupate, usually at the bottom of the pool and emerge as dull coloured, moth-like insects with greyish or brown wings.

Chemical control is virtually impossible owing to the protective structures which these pests construct, but an adequate stock of fish will keep the population down, as they consider the succulent larvae a great delicacy.

False Leaf-mining Midge

The False Leaf-mining Midge, *Cricotopus ornatus*, is a pest which makes an occasional appearance. Its minute larvae eat a narrow tracery of lines all over the surface of the foliage of floating-leafed aquatic plants which eventually turns brown and decays. Forcible spraying of the foliage with clear water is the best control, although in the absence of fish a nicotine spray usually proves to be effective.

DISEASES

Waterlily Leaf Spot

Two leaf spot diseases commonly affect waterlilies in this country. *Ovularia nymphaerum* appears as dark patches on the foliage, which rots through and causes the eventual disintegration of the leaves. It is always prevalent in a wet summer and as soon as noticed, affected leaves should be removed and burnt.

The other leaf spot, various *Cercosporae* species, is not quite as common, but equally destructive. The foliage becomes brown and dry at the edges, eventually crumbling, and wasting away. Removal and destruction of all diseased leaves is the only effective cure, although a weak solution of Bordeaux mixture sprayed over the foliage is often recommended for checking its spread.

Waterlily Root Rot
A root rot of the genera *Phytophthora*, sometimes affects water-lilies; those with dark mottled foliage seeming particularly susceptible. The leaf and flower stems become soft and blackened and the root becomes evil-smelling and gelatinous. Affected plants must be removed immediately and destroyed, and the others protected by impregnating the water with copper sulphate at 2½ ozs to 10,000 gallons. The copper sulphate crystals should be tied in a muslin bag to the end of a stick and dragged through the water until completely dissolved. All fish must, of course, be removed prior to this treatment.

PART THREE

FISH AND OTHER LIVESTOCK

(9)

Fish for the Pool

A well-planted pool is like an artist's canvas, the cool glassy still-ness framed with rushes, just waiting to be transformed into some-thing colourful and exciting or pale and restful. The touch of the brush is the addition of fish, bright red goldfish, multi-coloured shubunkins or salmon-pink carp, or maybe the slender orange-pink golden orfe, tiny grey minnows or exotic black moors. These are the ones, comparable with the artist's colours, which can be mixed or blended together to give the desired effect—bringing the canvas to life. Not only visual life, but also in a practical manner by assisting considerably in maintaining a natural balance.

As will be readily appreciated by those of scientific inclination, submerged plants in the presence of sunlight absorb carbonic acid gas produced by fish and other aquatic creatures. In conjunction with the green colouring matter or chlorophyll in the leaves of these plants it is then converted into nutriment. During this pro-cess oxygen is produced from tiny 'pores' concentrated on the undersides of the leaves and dispersed into the water for the benefit of the fish. Therefore, for the general well-being of each other, it is desirable to have a quantity of both plant and animal life in the pond and with such a multitude of varieties to choose from, what better animal life to choose than fish!

Ornamental fish should not be introduced into a newly established pond until a couple of weeks after planting, as they invariably root about amongst the plants, disturbing them and retarding their growth considerably. If planting has been done in containers then one can sometimes get away with introducing fish and plants together, but this is not really advisable. As with all projects involving mother nature, patience is the primary ingredient for success.

Much nonsense is talked and written about the stocking rate for fish in a garden pool. Six inches length of fish inclusive of tail to every square foot of surface area, except in the tiniest of pools is the maximum at which fish will live happily. However, in the initial stages of establishment this rate is not generally recommended for two reasons. Firstly most pool-owners like to watch their fish grow, which they would be unlikely to do at the maximum rate, and secondly where breeding is envisaged even on a modest scale a maximum rate would tend to lead to casualties, especially amongst young fry. Initial stocking at about a quarter of the maximum (i.e. one and a half inches per square foot) would seem to be the most satisfactory.

ORNAMENTAL FISH

The following ornamental pond fish, with the exception of catfish (see page 167), will all mix quite happily with one another. None has aggressive or cannibalistic tendencies and even young fishes, once they are past the fry stage and recognisable as fish, will mix happily with all sizes and both sexes of the species discussed. In only a few cases are the ultimate size of the adults given as these vary according to environment. All fish, no matter what species, grow in accordance with their surroundings. That is why a goldfish confined to a round bowl for a number of years retains its small size, yet once introduced to a pool will grow rapidly and attain quite sizeable proportions.

Bitterling

Although generally regarded as a coldwater aquarium fish, because it is only under such conditions that its extraordinary habits can be observed, the Bitterling or Bitter Carp *Rhodeus sericeus amarus* is also a useful and attractive subject for the pool. With the general appearance of a small carp, but with a lustrous metallic sheen, this tiny fellow is an exceedingly active individual that can be more readily appreciated in the smaller pool. Neither male nor female normally exceed three inches in length and both are notoriously short-lived—seldom more than four years—but even in the tiniest of pools they can generally be induced to breed and provide continuity.

The male is a very distinctive and handsome creature with nuptial turbucles on its snout and about its eyes and a body coloration of intense blue and mauve which persists throughout the breeding season. The female is slightly duller and plain and produces a long ovipositor, often longer than the fish itself, which it uses to deposit its eggs in the mantle cavity of a living mussel, preferably the Painters Mussel, *Unio pictorum*. This it does two or three at a time, after which the male fish ejects its milt and the sperms are carried into the mussel through the inhalant siphon to fertilise the eggs. Incubation takes place within the mussel and lasts about three weeks. The young bitterling remain with their host for some time, leaving it only when they are capable of leading an independent life.

Bronze Carp

In most cases the fish sold as bronze carp are difficult to classify as a particular species, but generally they are uncoloured goldfish *Carassius auratus auratus*. Occasionally they are hybrids between the Common, Crucian and Scale Carps but more usually the former. Bronze Carp are a cheap and useful fish for stocking large expanses of water, but their introduction into a pool with coloured goldfish cannot be unreservedly recommended if breeding is envisaged, for the uncoloured version of the goldfish will interbreed with the good coloured kinds and, being dominant, will produce an abundance of bronze carp and very few conventional goldfish.

Common Carp

The Common Carp *Cyprinus carpio* and its various forms are excellent subjects for medium and larger size garden pools. Providing colour and diversity of shape, these cunning and somewhat playful fish bring a pond to life, adding something inexplicable which the common goldfish lack.

The original Common Carp which it is believed only occurred in the rivers Danube and Tisa has been so widely distributed and hybridised by man that the fish which we have today is barely recognisable from that of its ancestors. Commercial stocks of Common Carp are generally of a chubby meaty fish with a deep body, evenly distributed fins and a narrow tapering head with strong lips and four pendant barbels. In shallow pools the body coloration is often somewhat silvery, whereas in deeper waters it is of a more bronzed coppery hue.

The Chinese Red Carp or Higoi is thought to be a variation of the common carp. In this form the colour is salmon or orange-pink but otherwise identical, except possibly that the head is a trifle more depressed. As with all members of the Cyprinus family, the Higoi can reach noble proportions in quite a short time when given plenty of space.

Of similar general appearance but with a more conventional bronze coloration is the Scale Carp. Here again the head seems somewhat depressed and disproportionately small when compared with the body.

Apart from the more conventional completely scaled carp, there is a range of variants with smooth or only partially scaled bodies. There are three basic kinds: the Mirror Carp or King Carp with a smooth body only partially and irregularly scaled, generally in the region of the head and tail or occasionally on the back, or if scaled in a lateral line, it is only sparsely so. The Band Carp which is readily distinguished by the fact that its scales are arranged in rows, one of which proceeds along the lateral line, followed by another row along the dorsal line, which can, and often does, have various irregularities. And the Leather Carp which is entirely devoid of scales except on occasions when individual ones appear below the dorsal part of the body or near the caudal or other fins. The normally characteristic lateral line is replaced in the leather carp by a narrow furrow.

Crucian Carp

The Crucian Carp, *Carassius carassius*, is a cyprinid fish closely related to the Common Carp *Cyprinus carpio* only differing visibly by the complete absence of barbels. In the garden pool it will interbreed with the Common Carp and its varieties, so if a pure breed is required the two species of fish should not be mixed. Generally

(Above) *Iris kaemp-feri*, the Clematis-flowered Iris of Japan.

(Right) *Iris kaemp-feri* Hokkaido, a beautiful pale blue variety lined and veined with maroon.

(Left) *Iris laevigata*, the **Blue** Water Iris.

(Below) *Ligularia clivorum* 'Orange Queen'; a handsome perennial for a damp situation.

the Crucian Carp is a deep bodied fish with a rich chocolate and bronze coloration lightening to gold or greenish yellow on the belly, although in shallow or turbulent water it takes on a paler hue and becomes a longer, more elongated shape. The fins have a reddish infusion which again intensifies or fades according to pool conditions.

Dace

This is a fish for the larger pool with well oxygenated water. Seldom can it be successfully accommodated in a small pool, for apart from its large oxygen requirements it is essentially a shoal fish and needs several companions if it is to be at all happy. The Dace, *Leuciscus leuciscus*, like the Orfe *Idus idus*, is a surface feeding fish and does much to keep down the insect population. Indeed in a sizeable pond on a warm evening the antics of dace rising to flies at the surface of the water are most entertaining to watch.

The Dace is a slim fish of a steely grey colour with a relatively large head and long cylindrical body. Young specimens look very much like Roach *Rutilus rutilus*, but lack the bright red eye so characteristic of that species. Commercial stocks of this fish are scarce, those being offered invariably being of native origin. It would therefore be worth noting at this juncture that wild fish or fish suspected of having been caught in a river should not be introduced into the garden pool without being quarantined for at least two months. All rivers are full of disease which many of the endemic fish are resistant to or live with, but once transferred to the relatively sterile conditions of the garden pond run riot amongst the unprotected inhabitants.

Gibel or Prussian Carp

This is a natural variety of the Crucian Carp *Carassius carassius* with a slimmer body and more forked caudal fin. It is generally referred to in technical circles as *Carassius carassius var.* or by some authorities as *Carassius auratus gibelio*. From its generic name one can well imagine that it will interbreed quite freely with the Crucian Carp and Common Goldfish *Carassius auratus auratus* when mixed in the confines of a garden pond.

Goldfish

There cannot be anyone who is not familiar with the Common Goldfish, *Carassius auratus auratus*. In its various shades of reds, pinks, yellows and orange it is probably the best known and most domesticated fish of all. For centuries the Chinese have kept and bred goldfish for both food and decoration, so that those which we can so readily purchase today are in all probability a wide depar-

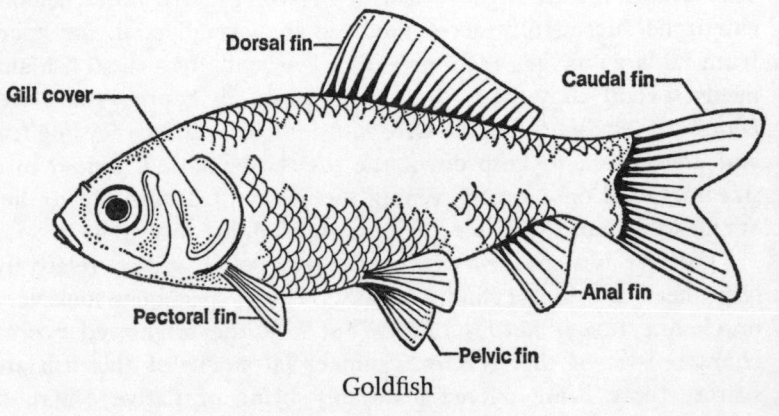

Goldfish

ture from the original species which once inhabited the rivers of China.

Apart from obvious differences in colour, the most striking divergence from the true goldfish is the production of a transparent scaled variety, the Shubunkin. In these, the body appears smooth and scaleless and in all manner of colour combinations. Reds, yellows, blues and violets intermingle and are often splashed and stained with crimson or black. From catalogues and books many pool-owners are led to believe that the Shubunkin is tamer and more friendly than the ordinary goldfish. Why should this be so if it is a mere variety of the goldfish? Are black or yellow humans any more friendly than white? I think not. They are merely colour variations of the same species and contain both friendly and un-friendly beings.

Apart from the wide and variable colour range exhibited by both Goldfish and Shubunkins, there are actual strains, particularly within the Shubunkins, which are very fine and breed true to character. Two of these are especially nice and worthy of special mention and the highest possible recommendation. The first is the Cambridge Blue Shubunkin, a fish with an even base of powder blue overlaid with violet and occasional patches of ochre, although these latter in the eyes of the connoisseur are undesirable. The other is the Bristol Blue Shubunkin, a strain developed by a group of fanciers in Bristol in which the base colour is again blue but heavily overlaid with violet and mauve and liberally splashed with crimson. Again in the expert's eye an excess of crimson or any colour other than blue is undesirable, but from an aesthetic point of view those that are splashed and stained with crimson or black are the most desirable. In this particular strain the dorsal and caudal fins are much larger and the lobes of the latter more rounded.

Varieties of all the preceding are available in Comet Longtail form. These are fish in which the tails are long and flowing, often as long as the body and give the appearance of a comet. In the blue forms of shubunkins previously described they are exceptionally fine and comparable with the most exotic tropical fish.

Fantails and Moors are varieties of goldfish with short dumpy bodies and tripartite tails. The Fantails have characteristic goldfish heads, while the Moors have somewhat bulbous telescopic eyes. Both forms occur in goldfish and shubunkins. The goldfish types of Fantail are known as Red or Red and White Fantails and the Shubunkin types as Calico Fantails. Moors fall into similar popular classes; the Shubunkins being known as Calico Moors, red goldfish types as Red Telescopes and the well-known black variety as Black Moors. The latter are exceptionally beautiful fish and worthy of special praise, their bodies being of the most intense and gorgeous velvety black.

Twin-tailed goldfish of the same general appearances as Fantails and Moors but with long drooping extended tails are generally known as Veiltails. By virtue of their excessive finnage they are slow swimming and ungainly when compared with the speedy Marilyn Monroe-like wiggles of their less favourably endowed counterparts.

Apart from possessing an extraordinarily long and fine pendant tail, the Oranda has a curious strawberry-like growth on the head. Otherwise it is identical to the typical bulbousless eyed veiltail. A further, and what one might consider final, departure from this is the Lionhead; a fish with similar strawberry-like excrescences on its head that call to mind a lion's mane and a short chubby body that is entirely devoid of a dorsal fin. However, there is one more variety that exceeds all others with its bizarre appearance and that is the one known as the Celestial. Its body is fairly typical of the conventional goldfish, but with a head that is flattened and bears two upward looking eyes that appear very much like headlights on a sleek sports car.

All goldfish and shubunkins are hardy in their natural forms, but many of the fancy kinds will not tolerate being frozen in the ice and unless a minimum depth of fifteen to eighteen inches can be provided at least at one point in the pool, then they are best avoided. Gardeners with more interest in the plants than the fish, or who through force of circumstances can spend little time with their pond should also leave fancy goldfish alone, for with their slow and ungainly manner of movement they are easy prey for all manner of diseases and natural predators. However, for the fortunate pool-owner with ample time to observe his fish and pander to their slightest whim, few can be so rewarding as the fancy varieties.

Gudgeon

Although I suppose this should strictly be classified as a 'scavenger' fish, most pool-owners keep it as a curio rather than for its scavenging habits. Once introduced into a pool it is seldom seen, preferring to live in the murky depths amongst the mulm in much the same manner as a tench. Gudgeon *Gobio gobio* are not particularly attractive fish either, having elongated somewhat cylindrical bodies, long tails and a large head with a pair of pendant barbels at the corners of the mouth. However, as intimated earlier they are useful bottom feeders and well worthwhile acquiring if not too expensive and from a reliable source. As with dace, stocks are not commonly available to the trade and those that are offered are often captured from the wild.

Koi Carp

The Koi carp appear to be hybrids between various members of the genera Cyprinus and Carassius, which have been evolved by the Japanese over many hundreds of years. Such has been the manner in which they have been bred, that special colour varieties have been produced able to breed to type. These have now become available in this country under a multitude of complicated Japanese names, such as *Shiro-ogon* white; *Sanke* white with red and black markings; *Ki-ogon* yellow and *Bekko*, tortoise-shell. Fanciful western names are now being given to these various different forms which are exceedingly popular amongst fish fanciers both in Britain and the United States. Indeed, as much as £3,000 has been known to have been paid for an especially fine specimen of a choice named variety. But coming down to earth, brightly coloured specimens of unnamed kinds sold by retailers in mixed batches can be obtained for as little as £1.50 for a three-inch fish. Even this may seem expensive to the uninitiated who is used to investing no more than 40p or 50p in a common goldfish, but the Koi is a creature of great beauty with an iridescent coloration and shiny mirror scales and, furthermore, has a certain scarcity value. Those of a lemon, golden or tangerine colouring are to my mind exceptional, but to the expert fancier, specimens containing dark and light grey, violet and white in a special patterning are the most desirable. Body shape is usually akin to that of the Higoi and growth rate similar, but often the familiar pendant bardels of that variety are absent.

Minnow

Our native Minnow *Phoxinus phoxinus* is a delightful little fellow for the garden pond. Although preferring shallow water and a stony bed it adapts well to life in captivity. It is, however, essentially a shoal fish—gregarious by nature—and to be really happy needs introducing in quantities of at least a dozen at a time. The coloration of minnows is very diverse, the basic colours being green and gold with a whitish or ochre belly. In the breeding season the males may be almost black with a reddish belly and crimson markings at the corners of the mouth. their flanks covered in dark spots and their heads in relatively large nuptial turbucles. For the remainder of the year they return to their somewhat drab colouring and appear as tiny flitting silvery darts amongst the 'lily' pads.

Orfe

The Orfe *Idus idus* (syn. *Leuciscus idus*) or Ide as it is sometimes called, is a handsome fish for the medium or larger pool. As with other shoaling fish it needs introducing in quantity if it is to be happy; and this it definitely is in well oxygenated water. The common species is known commercially as the Silver Orfe, a long slender fish with a small blunt head and obliquely cleft mouth. It seldom seems to breed successfully in captivity in this country, which is particularly mystifying as almost all commercial stocks originate from Germany where it apparently breeds quite freely under similar conditions.

The Golden Orfe is a variety of the species with deep orange-salmon body and silvery belly. Like its brother it is a fast growing, shoaling fish which delights in swimming just beneath the surface of the water and leaping and snatching insects from the air.

Roach

A native of slow moving rivers in Britain and throughout temperate Europe, the Roach *Rutilus rutilus* can be successfully adapted to pond life. As with dace and gudgeon stocks of dubious origin should be avoided, but several specialist suppliers are able to offer pond bred specimens which are ideal for the garden pool. Generally speaking the roach is of similar appearance to the Dace *Leuciscus leuciscus*, possibly a trifle meatier, but of the same steely grey colour. It is not so much a shoal fish, preferring the middle zone of the pond rather than the surface and in addition possesses bright red irises to the eyes all of which render it readily distinguishable from any other similar species.

Rudd

One of my favourite fish is undoubtedly the Common Rudd *Scardinius erythrophthalmus* and its silver and golden colour forms. Not only are they attractive in appearance but always swim close to the surface and, being almost exclusively vegetarian, graze voraciously on troublesome blanketweed. The typical species has a slender silvery-grey body and bright red fins, the dorsal one being situated much nearer the tail than in most other cyprinid fishes. In larger garden ponds with plenty of submerged plant growth, the various forms of rudd breed quite readily if left undisturbed and to their own devices.

SCAVENGING FISH

Although ornamental fish in their own right, those known commonly as 'scavengers' are seldom seen and generally introduced solely because of their scavenging nature and not their aesthetic qualities. Therefore I have seen fit to separate them from the main body of the text in order to assist the reader.

Scavenging fish in general are of immense value in clearing up accumulated debris on the floor of the pool—uneaten goldfish food, etc.—but will not, as many people assume, devour mud and stones or completely clear a pool of green slime and algae.

Catfish

The Horned Pout *Ameiurus nebulosus*, Brown Bullhead *Ictalyrus nebulosus* and the German Wels or Waller *Silurus glanis* are generally sold in this country by dealers under the collective name 'catfish'. All three species are superficially alike, having long barbels or whiskers, and similar habits—scavenging and feeding on all manner of aquatic insect life. However, none of the species can be unreservedly recommended for the garden pool as once of adult proportions they generally turn their attention from worms and insects to young fry and the tails of fancy goldfish such as comet longtails and fantails, shredding them beyond recognition. All fish that are sold under the collective heading of 'catfish' should be regarded with caution and only introduced to a pool where there are large fish and breeding is not envisaged.

Tench

The Green Tench *Tinca tinca* is undoubtedly the most popular and familiar 'scavenging' fish. With its short broad olive-green body and narrow tapering head it is a most distinctive character not easily confused with any other species. Like other scavenging fish once in the pond it is seldom seen again, preferring to lurk on the bottom where it can devour all manner of aquatic insect life, small plankton, uneaten goldfish food and other undesirable matter. In the garden pool, tench seldom breed successfully. This is curious as they, like goldfish, are members of the carp family and require similar conditions to those of their more amenable and prolific cousins. However, for those with determination for success, male and female can be readily identified once they have attained a length of six inches or more, for in the male the ventral fin invariably becomes larger and stronger often reaching as far as the anal orifice whereas in the female it remains short and weak.

Apart from the native species there is a mutant with a beautiful golden bronze coloration comparable with that of a goldfish or Higoi carp. However, as tench are seldom seen after being put in a pool, and as Golden Tench are at least three times as expensive as the common kind, to my way of thinking their introduction to anything other than the coldwater aquarium is a waste of money.

SELECTING THE FISH

Selecting the fish is undoubtedly more important than choosing plants, for with plants a miserable looking or misshapen specimen can often be coaxed into something worthwhile, whereas a fish that starts life in a similar way will in all probability remain miserable and misshapen. I am, generally speaking, against the purchasing of fish by mail order as one cannot choose particular colours, has little idea as to the health of the fish prior to their departure so that if they look unhappy on arrival it is difficult to ascertain whether it is the journey or a general malaise, and finally one has no claim against the supplier for losses in transit as live fish are always despatched at purchaser's risk. I do not for one minute doubt the honesty and integrity of mail order fish suppliers, but unless one lives in a remote or out of the way place, I would unhesitatingly recommend the purchasing of fish by sight at a local specialist's, even if it is only the local pet shop.

Most retailers of coldwater fish keep them in large fibre-glass tanks or conventional aquariums, the individual fish being graded according to size and variety. If the fish are in tanks with constantly flowing water (not merely recirculated) and with an overflow pipe and drain, they should be regarded with a certain amount of caution. For although this is a common method of containing a relatively large number of fish in a confined space it can lead to trouble for the purchaser when he gets his charges home. The idea behind this method of storage is to keep the water well oxygenated and wash away the free swimming White Spot parasite. However, the constant introduction of fresh turbulent tap water leads invariably to the breaking down or reduction of body slime on the fish, which in turn leaves it wide open to disease once introduced to the static and relatively impure water of the garden pond.

Fish swimming around peacefully in a static tank or one with a circulating or air pump operating are generally in better condition, especially if the water is mature and a little greenish or amber.

Most coldwater fish sold in this country today are imported. The common goldfish and shubunkins come from Italy, Golden Orfe from Germany and the fancy goldfish and Higoi and Koi carp from Japan, Singapore or Hong Kong. The fact that they have come, often, from tropical climates does not have any affect upon their hardiness or suitability for the outdoor pool in any way. However, it is a wise purchaser who enquires as to how long the fish have been in the country, or at least on the vendor's premises. Anything over a week is satisfactory as by then most varieties of fish have settled down and the travel weary ones succumbed. If one doubts the word of the vendor it can be assumed that the brighter the colour, especially with goldfish, the fresher the stock. I would always favour the purchase of a pale red or salmon-coloured fish rather than one of brilliant scarlet, as the former will almost certainly have been in the tank longer and therefore in better condition to face the ordeal that a journey involves. The same applies to shubunkins and to a lesser extent Golden Orfe, but does not seem to be quite the same with fancy carp who retain their colour whatever the conditions.

Green Tench should preferably be of a greyish colour. Never purchase dark coloured fish from a batch of greyish or olive-green ones as they will almost certainly be dead the following morning.

For some unaccountable reason a tench in its death throes turns very dark, almost black, and generally swims on his own and often just beneath the surface of the water. Catfish perform similarly and again it is advisable to choose those of a lighter blue.

All fish, no matter what variety, have stiff erect fins when they are in good health and this is the best indication the layman can have as to their well-being. Lively fish are not necessarily healthy but more often than not just hungry. It is an old dealer's trick to keep the fish hungry so that they will swim and dart about in search of any tasty morsel there might be and therefore appear livelier than they might usually be, and at the same time prevent the normal, not inconsiderable, fouling of the water. With small fish it is important to see that there are no damaged or missing scales as the exposed tissue is very susceptible to fungal infection. The same applies with larger fish, although the more ample the fish the less likely it is to discover one that is entire.

Generally, commercial ornamental fish are moved from place to place crowded together in large polythene bags with little water and thus are very susceptible to damage in transit. However, being larger and stronger any slightly damaged fish that contracts a fungal infection soon shakes it off if treated promptly with a proprietary fungus cure such as methylene blue or malachite green. In fact, it is advisable to give all newly purchased fish a dousing in a solution of either chemical as a disease precaution before introducing them to the pond. The manufacturer's instructions regarding rate of dilution should be followed carefully.

Occasionally white spots like tiny raised pin heads may be noticed on the bodies of the fish. These are invariably associated with the unfortunate but prevalent Ichthyophthirius or White Spot disease. Although curable (see page 197) it is inadvisable to purchase fish from any tanks on the premises until it has been cleared up, as once it is noticeable in one tank it is almost sure to be in the others transferred on a net or even by hand. However, the White Spot or Ich should not be confused with the nuptial turbucles which appear in profusion on the gill plates, head and sometimes front or pectoral fins of normal healthy male fish.

Apart from this, there are few other points to consider. Matters appertaining to the shape of the fish are purely personal. I like a fish to look like a fish and be of a conventional shape, but others disagree and prefer hybrids with bulbous eyes or tripartite tails, but this is dependent entirely upon personal whim. However, when purchasing tench, it is wise to look out for deformity in the backbone and in carp the condition known as 'Big Head'. The latter appears especially in Mirror and Leather carp and is recognisable as an ordinary but slightly oversized head surmounting a slim somewhat 'pinched' body. Nobody seems to be clear as to what brings about this condition, but it almost invariably leads to premature death.

Most suppliers pack fish in heavy gauge polythene bags with a little water and occasionally blown up with oxygen. Fish travel quite happily in these as a rule, but it is advisable to insist on large specimens being packed individually, and never to purchase surface swimmers such as orfe or rudd on a hot or humid day. Under warm conditions the latter rapidly deplete the water of oxygen and do not travel very satisfactorily.

When introducing fish into a pond float the bag on the surface of the water with the end still fastened until the temperature of the water both inside and outside is approximately equal. The fish may then be gently poured out. With fish that have travelled overnight by rail the same procedure applies, but a meal shortly after their arrival is much appreciated as they will have been starved for a couple of days before despatch to ensure that they do not foul the water in the bag excessively whilst in transit. On introduction, new arrivals are often nervous and shy, hiding amongst the weed and beneath the lily 'pads', but after three or four days they settle down and are soon swimming about quite happily.

OTHER LIVESTOCK

Apart from fishes there are a number of other aquatic creatures of value in creating harmony within the pool. These are mainly molluscs of various types—snails and mussels. Snails of certain species are useful in that they devour rotting vegetation and algae of various kinds, especially the soft filamentous varieties that cling to the walls of the pool. They are also a good indication of water hardness, for in waters with a high pH value their shells are smooth and shiny, whereas in soft acid waters they become badly pitted and very brittle. Mussels similarly perform a cleaning function, in that they act as filters sucking in and blowing out water, retaining all manner of minute suspended life such as free-floating algae in the process.

Freshwater Mussels

As indicated previously, freshwater mussels are valuable in clearing the water of small green suspended algae. However, they really only have a noticeable effect when in quantity and in pools of considerable volume. In small pools they are inadvisable as the water often becomes too warm for their liking or else there is insufficient mulm on the bottom in which they can bury themselves and should they expire the pollution caused by the putrefying remains will contaminate the water to an unbelievable degree. The repellant odour of a skunk is akin to that of sweet violets compared with the stench emanating from a decaying mussel.

The common Swan Mussel *Anadonta cygnea* is the species usually available. This is a dull brownish-green shelled variety, roughly oval in shape and containing a white fleshy body. Most commercial specimens are two inches or so long, but they can attain a length of some four or five inches after a number of years in favourable conditions.

The only other species worth consideration or indeed commonly encountered is the Painters' Mussel *Unio pictorum*, a more diminutive fellow with a yellowish-green shell marked liberally with dark brown growth rings. Although from the average pond-keeper's point of view, the swan mussel is superior owing to its greater effectiveness per specimen, it is the Painters' Mussel that is essential as a host if one wishes to breed Bitterling (see page 158).

Freshwater Snails

Although there are a multitude of different species suitable for the garden pool, and coldwater aquarium, only the Ramshorn Snail *Planorbis corneus* is commonly recommended or available commercially. This has a somewhat flattened shell which the creature

carries in an upright position on its back. There are red fleshed
P. corneus var. rubra and white fleshed *P. corneus var. albus*
varieties in addition to the typical species which is black. All three
are hardy, but it is the black one which is the most economical
to use for stocking. Unfortunately if red, black and white are
introduced into the same pool or tank for the sake of variety, the
black during the course of breeding, will dominate the other two
colours which in a couple of generations will disappear. As most
people are aware snails are hermaphrodite—bisexual—but are
unable to, or rarely, fertilise themselves. In addition, one mating by
a snail is sufficient for several batches of eggs which, if a black snail
is in the parentage, will mean that for a number of generations the
young produced will be predominantly black.

Eggs of Planorbis species are laid on submerged plant life in flat
sticky pads of jelly about half an inch in diameter. They are much
sought after by fish as a delicacy, which explains why overpopula-
tion by these most prolific creatures seldom occurs, although
sufficient usually escape the ever open jaws of the fish and come
to maturity to assist with the general balance and replace inevitable
deaths.

Another snail not infrequently offered for sale as a suitable pond
variety is the Great Pond Snail *Limnaea stagnalis* and while this is
perfectly suitable for large expanses of water it only brings trouble
when introduced to the average garden pool. Apart from the
unfortunate fact that it is an intermediary host for a fish disease
passed in a circle by the seagull via the snail to the fish, it has
an infuriating habit of ignoring algae in the pond and turning its
attention to waterlily pads and broad leafed oxygenating plants,
converting them into unsightly holey scraps of vegetation. If these
snails have entered the pool by accident, either on plants or by
some other agent, then they can be captured by floating a lettuce
leaf or old cabbage stalk on the surface of the water. After twenty-
four hours the leaf or stalk with the snails clinging to it can be
removed and destroyed.

Limnaea stagnalis is an easily recognisable species with a tall
spiralled and pointed shell an inch or two high, and a fleshy greyish-
cream body. It lays eggs in the same manner as Planorbis, but

in long cylinders of jelly which can often be detected on the under-sides of lily 'pads'.

Two other species of a slightly less destructive nature can also be used as scavengers in a pool; the Ear Pondsnail *Limnaea auricularia* and the Wandering Pondsnail *L. peregrina*. Both generally restrict themselves to useful pursuits and can occasionally be purchased from aquatic suppliers. They are native species differing only from *L. stagnalis* in their smoother less twisted shells, smaller size and additionally with *L. auricularia*, the presence of an extra large aperture.

The Fountain Bladder Snail *Physa fontinalis* is like a diminutive form of *L. auricularia* but with a left-handed twisted shell and a short fleshy body with slender feelers. This is invariably a nuisance in smaller pools, puncturing the leaves of waterlilies and gnawing at the edges until eventually they crumble and disintegrate. Although they are seldom introduced deliberately, most pools have a complement of these creatures. In small volumes of water they should be captured and destroyed by the lettuce leaf method mentioned earlier, before defoliation of all the floating leaf plant population.

Frogs, Toads and Newts

Frogs, toads and newts often find their own way into a garden pond without being introduced, but seldom are all or even two located in the one pool. In fact where one occurs naturally, even the introduction of another class in considerable numbers does not seem to oust the indigenous population and the immigrants gradually fade away.

In Britain we are not over-endowed with a variety of amphibians, but those that do occur naturally are fascinating creatures and worth encouraging to stay in the pond in moderate numbers Writers in the past have condemned the keeping of frogs on the grounds that a male frog has been known to attach itself to a fish during its breeding season, clasping it around the gills from behind in typical breeding stance and causing considerable damage. However, the likelihood of this happening is remote, as a male frog will only perform this distasteful act in the absence of a partner.

FROGS: Three species of frog occur in this country, but only the Common Frog *Rana temporaria temporaria* is native, as the Edible form *R. esculenta* and the Marsh form *R. ridibunda ridibunda* were introduced in 1837 and 1935 respectively. The last two are also of very local distribution, the Marsh Frog being confined almost exclusively to Romney Marsh in Kent. All three are superficially alike, being a muddy green colour which varies according to the creature's background. However, the Edible Frog has a distinctive pale stripe down its back and the Marsh Frog, being the largest European frog, exceeds the length of the common variety by quite two or three inches attaining a length of some ten inches when fully outstretched.

Adults of all three species breed during spring or early summer, the common kind generally being the first to be roused by the call of spring. They enter the water and remain there for several days, the male embracing the female from behind and hugging her tightly with the assistance of sticky nuptial pads on his thumbs. When amplexus, as this act is more correctly known, is completed, the female deposits her spawn into the water whereupon the male ejects his sperms into the mass. Fertilisation completed, the jelly-like masses with tiny black spots are slowly transformed into tiny tadpoles. At first the tiny tadpoles feed on algae but as they metamorphose their taste changes and they become almost exclusively carnivorous. At this time, their tail begins to be absorbed and tiny legs develop until at about three months old they are replicas of their more substantial parents. After three or four years they are capable of breeding.

TOADS: Toads live a similar life to frogs and breed in an almost identical manner. However, they are mainly nocturnal and not quite as attractive as their cousins, although probably of more value in that they eat larger quantities of garden pests such as slugs, caterpillars and beetles. Toads differ from frogs in appearance, having a somewhat dry warty skin and an ungainly walking habit quite clearly distinguishable from the frogs' energetic hop. Two toad species occur wild in Britain, but in few places are either abundant. The largest is the Common Toad *Bufo bufo bufo*, a dull olive or brownish creature some six to eight inches long; however, his cousin the Natterjack *Bufo calamita* is most handsome, having a yellowish or orange stripe down its back.

NEWTS : Despite the universal fascination of frogs and toads it is the newts which are my favourite amphibian additions. Mistaken by many for lizards, these amazing creatures look like miniatures from a pre-Devonian world when hideous reptiles walked the earth. The Great Crested Newt *Triturus cristatus cristatus* in particular looks like a character direct from the realms of science fiction with its long tapering crest and black and yellow body. It grows up to eight inches long, but unlike its more sombre cousins spends the greater part of each year in the water.

The smaller Common Newt *T. vulgaris vulgaris* and tiny Palmate Newt. *T. helveticus helveticus* being more terrestrial are possibly of slightly less interest to the pond-keeper, but during spring delight the patient observer with their fascinating courtship dances. In these, the male contorts his body and flicks his tail violently for several minutes before depositing a spermatophore which is taken up by the female into her cloaca. The sperms from this then travel along the oviduct to fertilise the eggs—which are then released individually and wrapped in the leaf of a submerged aquatic plant —some five or six days later. Breeding takes place during spring and often extends into summer, but by the end of July the adults of both the common and palmate species have climbed out on to the land. They then take to hiding under stones and in similar damp places, remaining hidden throughout their winter hibernation.

The Common Newt and Palmate Newt are both of a similar brownish or olive colour. However, the male of the former displays a splendid wavy crest along his back, whereas the male Palmate Newt has a low straight crest and webbed toes. The females of both species are not crested and have less brightly marked whitish or pale orange bellies than their male counterparts.

Pond Tortoises and Terrapins

Surprisingly few people have heard of the existence of hardy species of these lovable lumbering reptiles, but at least five different kinds are tolerant of our erratic climate and will successfully winter out-doors. All will live happily in the average garden pool and should not upset the balance or way of life of the other inmates to any degree. Whilst it is true that a number introduced to a small pool will trample down plants and generally stir things up, a pair will make very little difference, except possibly for consuming an odd tiny or ailing fish; a small price to pay for the immeasurable pleasure they undoubtedly give.

Many specialist books advocate fencing the creatures in and providing an island for them to bask on, but from personal experience I have found both these unnecessary as they seldom wander more than a few yards from the pool—unless of course there is a large alternative expanse of water nearby—and always seem capable of scrambling onto the bank via the marginal shelf when such is present. All species feed on worms, leeches, beetles and small fish if left to their own devices, but with a little patience can be made lazy and docile by feeding regularly with canned cat or dog meat of any proprietary brand.

The commonest and most readily available species is the European Pond Tortoise *Emy orbicularis*, a black or deep brown 'shelled' variety with conspicuous yellow spots. The black head and clawed feet are also liberally splashed with yellow, whilst the long whip-like tail is almost exclusively black. When fully grown the carapace or shell is eight inches or so long.

A widely distributed native of north Africa, the Middle East, Italy and central Europe (and allegedly also formerly of Great Britain) this handsome fellow is the most attractive of the hardy species. Occasionally a female lays one or two eggs, or rarely up to a clutch of twelve, and although they are often the cause of much excitement in the local press, they are seldom fertile. However, few people on seeing the soft shelled oval egg nestling in the margin of their pool, can leave it without at least attempting to raise a young tortoise. The egg or eggs should be kept in a box of moist sand in a temperature of 70°F, possibly in the airing cupboard or somewhere similar. After several weeks, should a young pond tortoise emerge he can be placed in a heated aquarium with the water temperature at about 65°F and with a raised sandy bank on which to crawl. Feeding should then consist of minced meat or chopped worms until the little fellow is large enough to be placed in the pool to fend for himself.

A similar species, the American Pond Tortoise E. *blandingii*, requires identical treatment and, if not so colourful, is even more hardy, often being observed swimming beneath a layer of ice that has formed on the pond during the depths of winter.

The Spanish Terrapin *Clemmys leprosa* is a different character altogether, appearing to be less aggressive and quite shy until familiar with his owner. After this, however, he becomes a most interesting pet, swimming just beneath the surface and popping his head up periodically like a periscope. The colour of the carapace is very variable, from a light olive green to almost black, but the legs and head of all variations are liberally marked with stripes of yellow.

A very near neighbour, easily confused with the Spanish variety, is the Caspian Terrapin *Clemmys caspica*, a slightly smaller creature with grey skin delicately marked with a tracery of yellow lines. Reeves Terrapin, *Geoclemys reevesii*, a native of China, Japan and most areas of the Far East, is of a similar size to the Caspian Terrapin, but with a dull brown carapace, yellow plastron and distinctive ridges down the centre of the carapace. Although a friendly and suitable inmate for the pool, this species seldom comes to hand, and when it does is often disproportionately expensive.

FISH FOR THE INDOOR POOL

Most of the fish suitable for stocking an indoor pool have been described earlier. However, please bear in mind when making a choice that the water of an indoor pool will be continuously warm and have a relatively low oxygen content. It would therefore be foolish to choose fish with high oxygen requirements such as Orfe, Dace or Rudd and equally unwise to select large or coarse fish like Mirror Carp, Bronze Carp or Green Tench, which do not feel kindly towards a warm environment and are not as pleasing to the eye as the different goldfish varieties. In fact I would think that an indoor pool should be stocked entirely with forms of the goldfish, for they are easy going, brightly coloured and therefore in keeping with the exotic vegetation of their surroundings and, of course, unlike tropical fish can tolerate a varying temperature range. The owner of an indoor pool has an excellent opportunity of keeping a wide variety of goldfish types under ideal conditions. Lionheads, Orandas, Fantails and Moors can be introduced and possibly the most fascinating of all—the Celestial—can be grown to perfection. Pearlscales, a fancy variety of goldfish with a great proportion of nacreous scales, are ideally suited to the indoor pool.

(10)

Fish for the Aquarium

The fish in their various forms and gay colours bring an aquarium to life flitting about amongst plants and rocks, lurking in the sand or pebbles on the bottom or else arguing furiously with the constant stream of bubbles from the airstone. All these antics can be observed and the habits and way of life of the various species compared in a manner which is impossible in a pool. The tropical species are probably the most interesting, as more can be kept in a small aquarium owing to their naturally small size, than is generally possible with the coldwater species, and almost without exception their life cycles and peculiar quirks are more extraordinary than anything to be observed in their coldwater cousins.

When choosing fish for an aquarium the general guide outlined earlier for the selection of strong healthy fish still holds true, however, slight variations and additional points to look for will be discovered by the specialist in a particular genus of fish, and any-one contemplating the study and care of one or more allied genera would be advised to purchase a book on the subject. There are many books ranging in size from a paperback handbook to a leather bound tome on all the popular and commercial genera and their allies within the tropical field, but literature on the coldwater sector is sadly quite sparse. However, if one applies common sense in conjunction with the knowledge derived from the keeping of pool fish, then a most satisfying and rewarding hobby will be embarked upon.

COLDWATER FISH

The majority of pool fish, if obtained in their small sizes, are excellent for the aquarium and indeed form the bulk of fish in coldwater tanks in this country today. However, there are a number of species that are on the borderline of hardiness which make interesting acquisitions.

Bass and Sunfishes
To the British aquarist the various varieties of Bass and/or Sunfishes Elassoma, Mesogonistius and Enneacanthos species sold commercially are very mixed and confused and given all manner of fanciful names. I would not attempt here to sort them out, but I would just extol their virtues as an aquarium fish. Most kinds have an almost iridescent coloration; blues, yellows, bronze and green mixing in all combinations and in spots, bands and dashes, creating a glittering kaleidoscope which during the breeding season is an awe inspiring sight. Unfortunately most species are carnivorous and pugnacious and best kept with those of their own kind, although small specimens of all species can be kept quite successfully with goldfish. All feed readily on a flaked food, but are partial to live daphnia, tubifex worms or an occasional earthworm. Breeding is possible in the confines of an aquarium, but not really advisable as the gravel and plants are disturbed considerably and unless plenty of space is available, fighting amongst the males may well occur.

Goldfish
Little need be said here about the advantages of goldfish in an aquarium, a brief outline of the different varieties available being given earlier, so it just remains for me to mention the use to which each kind is best suited. Generally small fish, not exceeding three inches in length, are the best to start off with. Large fish generally wreck the plants and aquascape of any but the largest of aquariums. Fancy kinds are the best sorts to keep, as in the confines of a tank their individual beauty can be so much more readily appreciated. For those contemplating a bowl, either for their own amusement or as a special separate venture for the children, then the Fantail type of goldfish is the one to select, for of all the available kinds this is the one best suited to such a restricted environment.

Medeka or Rice Fish

The Medeka, *Oryzias latipes*, are easy going fish for the coldwater tank, mixing happily with the majority of other coldwater subjects and breeding readily in captivity. They are small fish, seldom more than an inch and a half long, and in commercial stocks are rich yellow or golden, a considerable departure from the olive colouring of the type. Breeding takes place more or less all the year round, but only when the water temperature is in the mid-seventies, the female carrying the ova around in a cluster from a narrow thread. After fertilisation they are brushed off onto the foliage of submerged plants. Feeding on a tropical or fine coldwater flake food is advisable and a supplement of live daphnia appreciated.

TROPICAL FISH

Although the ideal is to have a tank for every different species of fish, this is often not feasible owing to space and expense, and in the living room one generally wants the aquarium to be a living picture with contrasting plants and a diversity of fish. In this case one has to settle for a community tank. This involves choosing suitable species to give a range of form and yet ones that are not aggressive towards one another. In selecting suitable inmates one has to be aware of not a few of the habits of the species contemplated, particularly as regards food, for those with special dietary requirements are quite unsuitable. Fish that are neither aggressive towards others or shy in strange company are what are needed, and those that attain similar adult sizes should be selected.

It is also worth mentioning that a more representative tank can be obtained by ensuring that different species use all the available levels of water. A tank full of bottom dwellers would not be particularly attractive nor an aquarium that consisted entirely of surface swimmers. Two or three fish of each species should be used, but only one should be a male, otherwise fighting may occur. It is wise to remember that when stocking, a sufficient allowance should be made for growth and that a crowded tank is more prone to disease than a sensibly stocked one.

Tropical fish are divided scientifically into two types; live-bearers and egg-layers. The former are usually the easiest for the beginner to keep and even breed successfully. At birth both male and female of a live-bearing fish look identical, but with the passing of time the anal fin of the male grows narrower but longer and thicker until all that remains is a spike-like organ known as the gonopodium. This in the normal position is directed backwards, but is capable of being moved forwards or sideways at will.

When mating, the male swims furiously around the female with his fins spread and displaying his finest colours. He then approaches her from behind and with his gonopodium pointing forward he inserts the tip into her vent. Spermatazoa are ejected and the eggs fertilised internally. For some three or four weeks the female retains the embryo fish, becoming somewhat distended, until birth takes place when myriads of young fish—up to two hundred in a mature adult—are expelled one by one usually tail first into their watery environment.

An interesting feature of most live-bearing species is that the female can store spermatazoa from the male for a considerable time, producing three or four broods of youngsters at monthly intervals until all the sperms have been used.

The egg-laying species are probably more familiar to the average person, with their mode of reproduction. In general this follows the pattern of the Cyprinid fish—carp and goldfish types—which have been mentioned earlier. Some variation is inevitable, as eggs hatch out more quickly or slowly and are sometimes deposited singly or in a cluster, but the basic routine is identical.

LIVE-BEARERS

Guppy

Even non-aquarists have heard of the Guppy, *Lebistes reticulatus*, such is its popularity. The males are extremely colourful and available in mixtures and shades of yellow, green, blue and red, while the females are of an uninspiring greyish hue. The males are generally smaller than the females, but neither often exceed an inch and a half in length. However, for their small size, they breed prodigiously, bearing up to six broods a year. Guppies of different forms have been developed over the years by expert breeders and now some really wonderful kinds are available to the aquarist. Those known as Veiltails have a tail as long as the body, widening towards the bottom and vividly splashed with all colours of the rainbow. Scarf-tails have long streaming tails like coloured ribbons; Sword-tails have developed tails in which the lower rays are extended and point backwards like a sword, and Double Sword-tails have both divisions of the tail in sword-like form.

There are many other shapes of tails and several different colour varieties. Gold Guppies have a gold ground colour splashed with the usual colours of reds and blues; Lace Guppies have a network of black circles enclosing various colours and De Gaulle Guppies which I have recently seen advertised in an American aquarist magazine— well I will leave those to your imagination. In fact the list of varieties is endless, but no matter what kind is eventually chosen it will be found that they are easy going and extremely valuable members of the community tank.

Mollies

All the members of the Molliensia are extremely peaceful and easy going fish. The original form known affectionately as the Mollie was of a greenish colour, but through breeding and selection black varieties have been evolved. These are basically from two species *M. latipinna* which has a tall sharply angled dorsal fin and *M. sphenops* distinguishable by its short and somewhat rounded dorsal fin. Neither kind exceeds three inches in length and are therefore dwarfed by their handsome cousin *M. velifera* which attains a length of some four to five inches. This is a striking fellow with a greenish body spotted with red and possesses a large erect dorsal fin. It is with this latter species that *M. latipinna* is crossed to produce those most showy and extraordinary of creatures, the Sail-fin Mollies whose dorsal fins, as the common name implies, are like small sails. In a community tank the mollies are quite happy, but the temperature must be high, around 80°F, and food always plentiful, even if only algae on the submerged vegetation, which they will graze on voraciously in the absence of dried food.

Mosquito Fish

Heterandria formosa is a native of the southern United States and the tiniest of live-bearers, seldom exceeding an inch in length, the males often not attaining that. The overall colour is olive-brown or off-coffee, and the belly a silvery colour. Both flanks are adorned with a dark horizontal stripe crossed by eight to twelve dark bars and there are two black spots bordered with red at the base of both the dorsal and anal fins. In a community tank with large fishes the mosquito fish is best avoided as at best it will result in bullying and at worst in being devoured. In any case adult fish only should be introduced to a community tank.

Platys

The Platys, *Xiphophorus maculatus* (syn. *Platypaecillus maculatus*), are popular little fish of excellent temperament. However, they are somewhat small, seldom exceeding an inch and a half in length, although the females can grow up to nearly two inches. By continuous and selective breeding several single colour and colour combinations have been produced with fanciful names such as Festival and Sunset. These range in colour from red to gold, black and blue and combinations of these and other shades. They are easy to feed, eating all manner of dried foods and graze freely on algae that collects on the plants. Under favourable conditions they breed quite readily.

Swordtails

The Swordtails, *Xiphophorus helleri*, are a good fish in a community tank, but only when in experienced hands, for they soon grow to a large size and tend to bully the smaller inmates. Novices would do well to study the Swordtails' habits in a separate aquarium before mixing them with other species as their continual busy and somewhat aggressive nature needs understanding fully if it is to be coped with in a community tank. Many colours such as reds, golds and blacks have been introduced by selective breeding, although the green of the common species is not unattractive. Swordtails are easily catered for with dried foods, but will turn their attentions to the fry of their own and other species if they should make an appearance.

EGG-LAYERS

Angelfish

The Angelfish, *Pterophyllum scalare*, is the symbol of the tropical fish world. Even the most disinterested person must know of its existence, such is its fame. Actually there are three different species, but *P. scalare* is the one commonly available. This has the typical round disc-like body with extensive dorsal and anal fins and in the common form is a silvery colour with several vertical black bars. Black Lace and all black varieties exist and are highly prized by their owners, but these are a considerable departure from the type and are the result of continuous line breeding.

Angelfish are not ordinarily pugnacious, but they are temperamental and some mope and refuse to eat, eventually dying for no apparent reason. Good dried foods occasionally supplemented by live daphnia or tubifex worms is all they require, and once happily settled will breed quite freely. However, the eggs are best removed from the tank on the foliage they are attached to and placed in a separate container, but the water must be continuously aerated to simulate the fanning action their parents normally provide with their pectoral fins during incubation.

Bronze Catfish

Every community tank should have a scavenger, for he performs the valuable function of animated vacuum cleaner, sucking up uneaten fish food and other debris that is likely to pollute the water. For this purpose one cannot do better than introduce a Bronze Catfish, *Corydoros aeneus* a peaceful fellow not at all like the villains described previously, although having a similar whiskery appearance. The general coloration is bronzy-green with a sagittate patterning along the flanks.

Cherry Barb

The Cherry Barb, *Barbus titteya*, is a small Cyprinid fish attaining a length of about one and a half inches which seems to thrive on a community life. When it is young it is a muddy brownish colour with a dark brown stripe running from tip to tail. When adult, however, this background colour turns to a coppery hue with occasional highlights of vinous red. Conventional foods suit this little chap admirably and breeding is easily undertaken in softish water, the young being easy to raise to maturity.

Dwarf Gourami

One of the most beautiful little fish available to the aquarist is the Dwarf Gourami *Colisa lalia*. It is easy to feed, not at all aggressive and the male displays a wondrous pattern of red and blue vertical stripes on a silvery background. Its gill plates are blue and all his fins deep red speckled liberally with electric blue. The female is of similar patterning but much paler, the stripes on her body only being in evidence in certain lights or with close observation. Breeding is easy, the eggs being laid in a bubble nest, but it is advisable to remove the female immediately this occurs.

Harlequin

The Harlequin, *Rasbora heteromorpha*, is a striking little fish of vivid pinkish-gold and distinctive black triangles on the flanks. In a community tank with fishes of similar size—say up to two inches —it is quite content and particularly attractive when swimming in a shoal. Its needs are small, feeding contentedly on ordinary dried food, and breeding readily in conditions to its liking. To breed harlequins successfully they should be introduced to soft peaty water and left to their own devices, the adults being removed as soon as spawning has taken place.

Neon Tetra

Most people who have at some time watched fish in an aquarium will recall seeing tiny silvery-grey and red fish darting to and fro with a flashing band of brilliant blue-green along their flanks, a band that is seemingly painted on with fluorescent paint, such is its brilliance. This is the Neon Tetra, *Hyphessobrycon innesi*, a friendly little chap whose darting antics and brilliant coloration give immediate sparkle to the life in an aquarium. Breeding in soft water in a separate tank is simple and feeding of normal adult fish on a good flaked food quite adequate.

Pencil Fish

The Pencil Fish, *Nannostomus anomalus*, is a curious little fellow who moves about the tank in jerky movements. In soft water the male develops intense colorations, the body glowing copper and the fins fiery red with startling blue tips. In ordinary community tank conditions the colours are more sombre, but nevertheless render this a most useful acquisition. Feeding on a fine food is essential as its mouth is quite tiny, but a good staple dried food diet would seem adequate.

(11)

Pests and Diseases

Fish in common with other forms of domesticated livestock have their fair share of ills. In the relatively sterile medium of a garden pool or aquarium they are particularly vulnerable, therefore if they are to remain in good condition it is desirable to maintain a high standard of hygiene and also to avoid introducing any fish, snails or plants from natural sources unless strictly quarantined.

PESTS

Anchor Worm

The Anchor Worm, although not strictly a worm but a crustacean, is a fairly common parasite on members of the carp family. Several species exist, but the one that is specific to goldfish and carp is *Lernaea carassii*, a destructive little character with a slender tube-like body about a quarter of an inch long and a barbed head which embeds itself in the flesh of its host causing unsightly lesions and tumour-like growths. Often they become covered in algal growth which gives them a very pronounced and sinister appearance.

Control is by capturing host fish, holding them in a wet cloth and then touching the parasites with a brush dipped in a 0·1% solution of potassium permanganate or in ordinary household paraffin. This kills the little creatures which can then be withdrawn with tweezers and the open wound dressed with an antiseptic disinfectant solution such as Dettol.

Dragonflies

All the forty-two species of dragonflies native to Britain have naiad or developing stages which are predatory on fish. As development of the naiads varies from species to species from one to five years, the problem they can constitute over this period of time can be well imagined. They are unpleasant looking creatures, rather like a small scorpion, and vary in colour from green and brown to grey. All their developing life is spent in the pool clinging to submerged and partially submerged aquatic plant life awaiting suitable prey to pass by. When a tasty morsel is noticed they shoot forward their 'mask' from beneath their chin. This 'mask' is like a pair of jaws with strong hooks which grip the unfortunate victim and then by virtue of their retractable nature bring food back to the naiad's mouth. Although dragonfly naiads of native species rarely exceed three inches in length, and can seldom devour a fish at one go, they can nevertheless inflict quite serious injuries. Control is unfortunately restricted to removal by hand every time a naiad is noticed.

Fish Louse

There are numerous species of Fish Lice or *Argulus*. These are parasitic crustaceans of a singularly unpleasant nature, clinging to the bodies and especially around the gills, of all kinds of fish life. Each species or group of species of fish appear to have their own louse, those infesting goldfish being quite different from those found on catfish. All look much the same, however, with a large flattened end and shell-like carapace with a small abdomen projecting, and feeler-like attachments at the anterior end that are used for attachment to the host. Males and females are almost identical, but it is the females alone that are parasitic.

By holding an infested fish in a wet net and dabbing the parasites with a drop of paraffin on a child's paint brush the pests are easily dislodged, but as the tissue beneath may have been damaged it is advisable to dip thus treated fish in a solution of malachite green—one part to nine parts water—before reintroduction to the pool.

Great Diving Beetle

Both the larvae and adult of the six or so native species of Dytiscus are carnivorous and prey freely on young fish. The commonest species and one usually referred to as the Great Diving Beetle is

Dytiscus marginalis, a handsome fellow barely two inches long
with a roughly oval hard chitinous body of dark brown with a
distinctive golden border. The larvae are something along the same
lines as the naiads of various dragonfly species, but rarely exceed
an inch and a half in length.

Diving beetles are splendid aviators, flying from pool to pool in
the cool of the evening and therefore virtually impossible to control.
All one can do is net and destroy any offending adults, as soon as
they are noticed, before they have an opportunity to reproduce.

Great Silver Beetle

Although the adult of the Great Silver Beetle, *Hydrous piceus*, is
vegetarian, the hideous looking larvae is not and will prey on all
manner of livestock, tadpoles, fishes and more especially snails.
Fortunately it is not a widespread species being confined more to
the southern counties of England and seldom noticed further north
than the border. The larva itself attains a length of some two and
a half inches and looks like an ungainly prehistoric monster. The
body is more or less sausage-shaped of a dark brown colour and has
three pairs of legs just behind the head which it uses for locomo-
tion, dragging its ugly body behind it. Control once again is very
difficult as the adults travel from pond to pond.

Hydra

These tiny freshwater polyps of somewhat octopus-like appearance
will be familiar to all who have studied biology at school and,
although harmless to any fish likely to be introduced into a pool,
they will attack and kill any small fry that might be produced.
There are three native species, *Hydra viridissima* which is a greenish
colour, *H. oligactis* which is brown and *H. vulgaris* which is
yellowish or occasionally grey. All spend their lives attached to
plants, capturing prey by means of stinging tentacles which paralyse
the poor unfortunate creature that they have ensnared. Their usual
diet consists of worms and water fleas, but as intimated earlier
they will attack fish fry.

Control is difficult as they are so small. Hand picking is impossible,
for although they are visible to the eye, once the plant on which

they are clinging is touched they virtually 'dissolve' into an indistinctive gelatinous mass, only to reappear when the plant is reintroduced to the water.

Unless they are being particularly troublesome, chemical control is not worthwhile, for it involves removing all livestock from the pool and then adding a teaspoonful of ammonia for every four gallons of water. This will have no significant effect upon the plants, but will successfully destroy all insect and similar life. A couple of days after treatment the pool should be emptied and refilled with fresh water. If infestation was severe this may need repeating several times before the fish can be safely reintroduced.

Leeches

There are eleven known British species of leech, all of which are harmful in some measure to fish and snails. The largest is the Horse Leech, *Haemopsis sanguisuga*, which can grow as much as six inches long, whereas the smallest *Helobdella stagnalis* is only three-eighths of an inch long.

However, it is the Fish Leech, *Piscicola geometra*, which is generally the most troublesome. In common with all other leeches it has numerous blind sacs within its body for storing blood which it sucks from its hapless victims. One gorging generally lasts for several months, and during this time it just lingers about harmlessly amongst water plants digesting its meal. All our native leeches are hermaphrodite, sometimes mating in pairs, but self-fertilising as well. They generally attach their eggs to water plants, although the tiny *Helobdella stagnalis* carries its eggs around beneath it.

Control is difficult, but a piece of meat anchored to a length of string and floated on the water over-night will attract considerable numbers which can then be removed and destroyed. Fish with leeches attached, can have them removed if held in a wet net or cloth and a dab of salt administered to the tail of the assailant; it will then immediately detach itself.

Water Boatmen

Two families of aquatic insects are known as Water Boatmen, the *Corixidae* or Lesser Water Boatmen, and the *Notonectidae*. How-

The Common Gold-
fish.

Celestial goldfish, an
exotic variety with
upturned eyes.

(Below left) Fantail
goldfish, a dumpy
variety with tripar-
tite tail.

(Below right) Black
Moor, a fine velvety
black departure from
the Fantail.

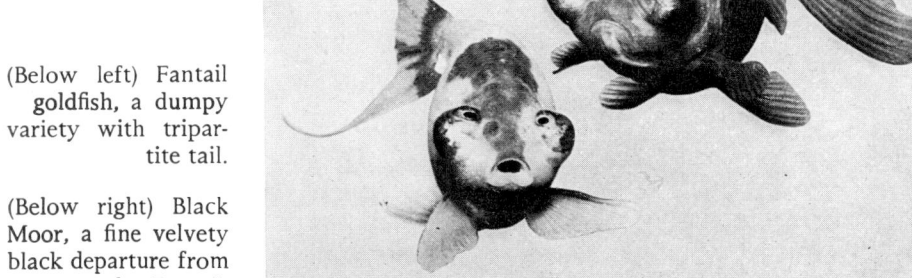

The Shubunkin, a **multicoloured transparent** scaled variety of goldfish.

Golden Orfe, a lively shoalfish.

The Nishiki Koi Carp, highly prized in Japan.

The Green or Common Tench, the most useful scavenger fish.

ever, it is only the latter that are harmful to life in the pond. They feed chiefly on aquatic insects, tadpoles and fish eggs but are also capable of killing or inflicting nasty wounds on small fish. The basic difference between the two families from the pond-owner's point of view is that the harmful *Notonectidae* swim on their backs whereas the *Corixidea* swim upright in a more conventional manner.

The commonest Water Boatman, *Notonecta glauca*, is a small roughly oval shaped creature about half an inch long with a black belly and pale brown back with a conspicuous triangular mark in the centre. Its legs appear like oars and propel the little creature through the water with great speed. Control is difficult and hand picking is the only method of ridding a pond of this nuisance and then it is only a temporary alleviation as they always seem to reappear within a couple of months.

Water Scorpion
There is only one species of Water Scorpion native to Britain and indeed Europe. This is *Nepa cinerea*, a vicious little character no more than an inch and a half long, with a strong pair of front legs in which it grabs its prey, and a hideous mouth piece which it uses to pierce and suck dry its victim. In appearance it is much like a very small brownish version of most people's idea of a conventional scorpion. The greater part of its life is spent sitting motionless amongst water plants or on the bottom awaiting suitable juicy morsels to pass by. It breeds during the spring, depositing relatively large eggs amongst decomposing plant remains or blanket weed and other filamentous algaes. Control is once again by hand picking, but they can be discouraged by general pond hygiene. A lack of blanket weed and decomposing foliage in which they can breed and hide makes life difficult for them.

Water Stick Insect
Although known as the Water Stick Insect, *Ranatra linearis*, is a member of the same family as the Water Scorpion and has similar habits. It is a very thin and slightly larger version of its cousin,

but can be controlled in the same manner. Pond hygiene keeps it at bay.

Whirligig Beetle
The larva of the Whirligig Beetle, *Orectochilus villosus*, is a small insect, barely three-quarters of an inch long, with a voracious appetite for other aquatic insect life and seeming love of attacking small fish. It is a dull insignificant yellowish-white colour and roughly cylindrical in shape with three pairs of legs near the head and several pairs of feathery appendages along its body. The adults are readily recognisable as little black rounded beetles which swim fantastically fast in circles or spirals on the water surface. They breed during May and June depositing eggs on the roots and submerged foliage of aquatic plants. Control of the larvae is really coupled with control of the relatively harmless adults which is once again by hand picking.

DISEASES

Dropsy
The condition known variously as Dropsy or Scale Protrusion is caused by bacteria of the genus *Pseudomonas*. Fish with this disease become distended with scales standing out from the body and one or sometimes more of their internal organs become filled with liquid. This can be drawn off with a hypodermic needle if one has a steady hand, but as the organs become rapidly refilled and the operation is tricky, it is only worth considering as a last resort when valuable fish are involved.

Control in commercial stocks of food fishes has been effected by injections of antibiotics, but as the latter is not generally available to the amateur as yet and the previous method advocated is of dubious merit, I think the easiest and kindest way to deal with dropsical fish is to destroy them before they become too badly distended and deformed.

Fin Rot (and Tail Rot)
Fin or Tail Rot is a fairly prevalent disease, but one about which little is known. Several bacterial organisms have been blamed

although the main culprit has not to date been isolated. The infection usually appears first in the dorsal fins, gradually spreading to the others and in severe cases reduces them to a mere stub.

The first noticeable sign of disease is the presence of a whitish line along the outer margin of the fin which gradually moves downwards leaving the outer margin badly frayed owing to the disintegration of soft tissue between the hard rays of the fins. If infection is allowed to creep as far as the body of the fish death usually ensues, but if an affected fish is noticed in time, the badly frayed fin tissue removed with a pair of scissors and the poor creature placed in a solution of one part malachite green to nine parts water and then replaced into the pool or aquarium the trouble is usually cleared up and the damaged areas almost invariably regenerate.

Fungus

Whenever a fish becomes damaged in any way, either as a result of colliding with a sharp rock or other object in the pool or aquarium, or else after suffering from some other malady such as White Spot, Anchor Worm or just mishandling, it is open to an attack by fungus. This usually appears as a greyish film or cotton wool-like growth on the open wound, occasionally spreading to, and invading, the gills and mouth. Trouble is caused principally by the aquatic fungi of the genus Saprolegnia and Achyla which attack not only living fishes but also damaged fish eggs and uneaten food, the latter of which points to the value of having scavenging fish in a pool and of a high standard of hygiene in the aquarium.

Fungal growth on large fish is relatively easy to clear up, but fry and small goldfish are very difficult and seldom worth the trouble and should therefore be destroyed immediately. Dipping infected fish in a solution of malachite green or methylene blue— which are usually the pet care manufacturer's proprietary brands of fungus-cure—strictly according to manufacturer's instructions soon detaches the fungal growth and prevents trouble recurring.

A salt bath can also be used with some measure of success, although it is generally long-winded. Rock, or preferably sea salt (never table salt), is dissolved at the rate of a tablespoonful to a gallon of water and the fish immersed in this for a couple of days. This solution can be increased gradually to a maximum of three tablespoons to a gallon of water until the fungus falls away, and then reduced slowly until normality is reached once more when the patient can be returned to the pool or aquarium.

Feeding fish with a food containing an anti-fungal ingredient such as saprolegnil does much to discourage the appearance of fungus and should it ever appear one can be sure the fish will be better able to stand the fungal onslaught than they might otherwise have been.

Gill Flukes

Gill flukes of the genera *Gyrodactylus* and *Dactylogyrus* are occasionally encountered in both pool and aquarium. They are very minute, impossible to see with the naked eye, but their presence is very evident when the fish appear to go crazy, rushing about banging themselves against the sides and rising to the surface in sudden fits. The rate of breathing of an infested fish is greatly increased and the constantly twitching fins are a clear indication of the gill fluke's presence.

Cures of various kinds with formalin and mild disinfectant solutions are often recommended but as at least fifty per cent of fish die during treatment, I would always advocate destroying affected inmates as soon as the trouble is diagnosed.

Red Pest

This is an uncommon but very infectious bacterial infection in which the fish become sluggish and rise to the surface. Patches of rusty red appear on the sides and belly, and occasionally on the anal and pelvic fins. All fish should be removed from the pool and the latter allowed to remain fishless for six or eight weeks. Unless valuable fish are involved it is better to destroy the entire stock and start afresh. If, however, valuable Koi or Higoi carp are affected, they can sometimes be cured by being kept in constantly running water.

Slime and Skin Diseases

Several parasites cause skin disorders and slime disease. All are simple one-celled organisms and of the genera Costia, Cyclochaete and Chilodonella. Fish that are affected with these organisms often scrape themselves against the bottom of the pool or aquarium usually have folded fins, and often turn bluish-white with a slimy deposit which it would appear is a combination of natural slime and the parasites.

Fish that are not too badly diseased can be bathed in acriflavine solution for two or three days, or a salt treatment as prescribed for fungal diseases (see page 195), with reasonable assurance of success. Badly diseased fish should be destroyed.

White Spot Disease

White Spot is a universally prevalent parasitic disease in fresh-water caused by a member of the group of single celled creatures known as Protozoa. The actual parasite is known as *Ichthyophthirius multifilis* or more familiarly to fish fanciers as 'Ich'. It is an extremely troublesome disease in aquaria where the water temperature is relatively high, as in raised temperatures the life cycle of the creature becomes accelerated and death becomes a much more rapid and inevitable thing. It can be equally pernicious in the garden pool, but with the lower water temperatures the life cycle is slowed down and treatment can be effected before too much damage has been caused.

Ichthyophthirius is not a particularly large creature, seldom as much as a millimetre across, but its presence for at least part of its life cycle imbedded in the skin of a fish does have considerable effect upon its host. Badly infested fish look as if they have white measles, generally take on a pinched appearance and swim in a drunken manner. Heavy attacks such as this are seldom curable and the best one can do is to despatch the poor unfortunate fish as soon as possible. If a light sprinkling of spots is noticed on the tail or fins of an adult fish then this is usually curable, but where odd parasites are noticed on fry, the young fish are best removed and destroyed as the presence of only a couple of these tiny assailants on very young stock inevitably leads to death.

Ich shows various stages of development which must be known in order to combat it effectively and with the utmost safety to the troubled fish. In the initial stages of growth the 'spores' or 'swarmers' are roughly pear-shaped and bore their way into the skin of living fish. Here they feed on their host until of adult size when they are visible to the naked eye as white spots.

The mature parasites leave the fish through a hole in the skin and then become free-swimming, eventually to become encysted. Inside the cyst they divide into upwards of a thousand 'spores' which leave the cyst as free-swimming creatures in search of another host.

From the foregoing one can appreciate that Ich can only be destroyed in the swarming stage. The white spots that are plainly visible on the fish are embedded in the skin and quite safe, so efforts have to be made to destroy the creature while it is still in the water. It is known that in a certain temperature range that the free-swimming stage must find a host within forty-eight hours or else perish, so therefore by removing all the fish to tanks or bowls of clean water and then changing from tank to tank each day, the free-swimming parasites can either be starved of fish life or washed away. When a pool is involved and the temperature of the water is obviously quite low, it has to remain without fish for upwards of six weeks as development of all stages can be very slow in these lower temperatures.

Apart from the clean water method, there are several chemical White Spot cures on the market that are quite effective. Most are based on an acriflavine solution, or else quinine salts such as quinine hydrochloride and quinine sulphate and, in particularly stubborn cases, a combination of acriflavine and methylene blue. Fish are kept in such solutions until all spots have left the skin, the free-swimming stage of the parasite then being killed by the chemicals. Several schools of thought exist as to the usefulness of chemicals, particularly quinine as it is thought to sterilise fish, but to date I have still to be shown some sound evidence to support this theory.

White Spot is unfortunately a widespread disease and there can be few garden pool owners or aquarists who have not experienced trouble with this menace at some time or other. However, much can be done to restrict the opportunity for its incidence by observing several precautions. Firstly, make sure that any fresh stock of fish is absolutely free of the visible signs of the disease before introduction to the existing community. If White Spot is suspected, quarantine the new purchases in a solution of quinine sulphate and raise the temperature to 65° or 70°F for a few days. If latent parasites are present they will soon emerge and break free. Secondly, never collect aquatic plants from the wild and introduce them to the pool or aquarium as these are often smothered with parasites. And finally, try to avoid topping up a pool with tap water, as White Spot cysts can often be found in this and chlorination does not seem to destroy them. August is the worst month for the disease being introduced this way as the reservoirs are low and the number of cysts to the volume of water is greater. Rain water is better, unless you have an assurance from your waterboard that there are no fish in the local reservoir, which is very unlikely.

OTHER DISORDERS

Cataract
Although not all that common, the cataract of the eye of a fish is deserving of passing mention. Affected fish have a white film covering the pupil which gradually spreads to envelop the entire eye. Drying the eye with a soft cloth or cotton wool and then dabbing with a mixture of iodine and glycerine in the ratio of one part to nine by volume generally cures the trouble, but requires doing regularly twice daily for several days before the film disappears.

Chlorine Damage
Most pool owners have to fill their pools initially and continue topping them up with tap water. Tap water, as most readers will appreciate, contains chlorine as a disinfectant for killing bacteria. In the quantities it is introduced in our water it can be harmful to fish, more especially young fry, and in large cold volumes takes a considerable time to disperse and evaporate. Fish damaged by chlorine show very pale gills with the edges bleached white and while damage to pool fish is not frequent, it is a problem to be

on the look out for especially if the pool has just been cleaned out and refilled. By leaving the water in the pool to stand for a week or so before the introduction of livestock this problem can be alleviated. However, if for some reason this is impossible, either add a small quantity of sodium thiosulphate or filter the water through activated charcoal to render it harmless. This latter method is particularly useful when setting up an aquarium.

Constipation
When a fish trails a stream of excrement from the vent, especially if interspersed with tiny bubbles, it is a sure sign of constipation. This condition is generally brought about by an unbalanced diet and if left untreated can lead to death or at best, distortion of the digestive tract. Starchy foods should be immediately withdrawn and the troubled fish fed on live foods and boiled chopped cabbage or spinach. If the condition persists or is in an advanced state when first noticed, the fish should be immersed for a few minutes each day in a solution of Epsom salts, the salts being dissolved at the rate of two and a half ounces to a gallon of water.

Loss of Balance
Fish that swim upside down, nose downwards or in a swaying or undulating manner are usually suffering from a condition known as 'loss of balance'. This is a physiological disorder which is usually brought about by a derangement of the swim bladder, or occasionally as a result of constipation. Various treatments are said to have some effect on fish not too badly afflicted and consist mainly of raising the water temperature, purging, and altering diets, but generally none of these are of a permanent nature and any fish that are seen obviously in distress should be quickly destroyed.

Spawn Binding
Spawn binding is a particularly unfortunate occurrence that is not infrequently encountered in fish that are kept in captivity. In their natural environment fish find it possible to spawn at will and in the normal period that their body dictates that they should, but in a small pool or aquarium this is often not the case and the eggs must

be dissolved and reabsorbed by the fish's body. When a female has been poorly nourished and in crowded unpleasant surroundings this reabsorbtion is difficult and the fattened eggs become hard and incapable of being expelled. These then decay within the fish and an accumulation of gas occurs which generally results in the death of the fish.

Stripping of the eggs as described on page 47 is sometimes successful, although where large numbers have become hardened within the body they are often difficult to expel without damaging the internal organs of the fish. A knitting needle or similar instrument suitably coated with an antiseptic grease such as Vaseline and then inserted in the vent parallel to the fish's body sometimes assists in their release, which follows by normal stripping methods.

Rather than attempting a cure, it is far better to prevent the occurrence of such a disorder by feeding fishes on a varied diet, including live and green foods if possible and seeing that they have ample space in which to move.

Tumours

Sometimes a tumour will be noticed on the body of an otherwise healthy fish, appearing as a hard raised lump. If this persists for several weeks and is definitely not the beginnings of an anchor worm infestation (see page 189), then the fish should be quickly destroyed. Although tumours can be removed with a razor blade, this is a major operation and the fish will seldom survive, or if it does will not be a very attractive specimen. If left alone, the tumour will almost inevitably bring about the death of the fish, so it is in the poor creature's interest to be despatched with all due haste.

Wasting

When fish look emaciated and have arched backs and pinched bodies, they are almost certainly suffering from old age. However, one cannot rely upon this diagnosis and it is advisable to destroy any badly pinched or deformed specimens, for the trouble could also be caused by the virulent and pernicious *Mycobacterium tuberculosis*, the instigator of Fish Tuberculosis. This is a form of tuberculosis, fortunately uncontractible by humans, for which there is no cure.

Wounds

With the best will in the world it is impossible to protect fish from all the hazards of their environment and it is inevitable that at some stage in their lives they will lose some scales, graze their body or damage their fins in some way. When this is noticed it is advisable to dress open areas with a mild solution of an antiseptic disinfectant such as Dettol and then coat with Vaseline before reintroduction to the pond or tank.

HOW TO DESTROY AN AILING FISH

Many dubious methods have been advocated by people I have come in contact with and one to which many subscribe is flushing the poor unfortunate fellow down the lavatory. This is rather inhuman as the fish is still alive and suffering from an ailment, only to be shot into a dark and unwholesome environment in which death will be painfully slow. Taking an unhealthy fish in a dry cloth and then dashing it smartly against a hard surface such as a concrete path results in instantaneous death.

Easy Reference Guide to Pool Plants

NYMPHAEA (WATERLILIES)

The measurements referred to are the ideal depths at which each variety succeeds. However, it does not follow that they will not grow with some degree of success at shallower or greater depths.

WHITE

Up to 1 ft	fennica	Up to 3½ ft	Marliacea Albida
	nitida	Up to 4 ft	odorata
	odorata var. minor		tuberosa
	tetragona		t. 'Maxima'
	t. var. leibergii		t. 'Paeslingberg'
	Pygmaea Alba		t. 'Richardsonii'
Up to 1½ ft	candida	Over 4 ft	alba
	caroliniana 'Nivea'		a. 'Plenissima'
Up to 2 ft	Albatross		Gladstoniana
	Gonnere		Goliath
	Laydekeri Alba		
Up to 2½ ft	Hermine		
	Virginalis		

YELLOW

Up to 1 ft	Pygmaea Helvola	Up to 2½ ft	Marliacea Chroma-
Up to 1½ ft	Paul Hariot		tella
Up to 2 ft	odorata sulphurea		Moorei
	o.s. 'Grandiflora'	Up to 3½ ft	Sunrise
	Solfatare	Up to 4 ft	Col. A. J. Welch

PINK

Up to 1 ft	odorata 'Exquisita'		o. 'Suavissima'
	Pygmaea Johann		o. 'William B.
	Pring		Shaw'
Up to 1½ ft	caroliniana		Arethusa
	Rose Nymph		Baroness Orczy

Up to 2 ft odorata 'Jessieana'
o. 'Luciana'
Laydekeri Rosea
Odalisque
Somptuosa
Up to 2½ ft odorata var. minor
floribus roseis
odorata var. rosea
o. 'Turicensis'
Amabilis
Marliacea Rubra-
Punctata
Mrs. Richmond
Newton

Esmeralda
Eucharis
Princess Elizabeth
Rose Arey
Up to 3 ft odorata 'Firecrest'
Brackleyi Rosea
Gloire de Temple
sur Lot
Masaniello
Up to 4 ft tuberosa var. rosea
Marliacea Rosea
Over 4 ft Collosea
Marliacea Carnea

RED

Up to 1 ft Pygmaea Rubra
Maurice Laydeker
Up to 1½ ft Vesuve
Up to 2 ft Comte de Bouchard
Conqueror
Ellisiana
Fabiola
Froebeli
Galatee
Graziella
Indiana
Laydekeri Fulgens
L. Lilacea
L. Purpurata

Up to 2½ ft odorata 'Rubra'
Marliacea Flammea
M. Ignea
Seignourettii
William Falconer
Up to 3 ft odorata 'Helen
Fowler'
Andreana
Gloriosa
James Brydon
Up to 4 ft Attraction
Charles de Meur-
ville
Up to 6 ft Escarboucle

CHAMELEON AND STRIPED

Up to 1½ ft Aurora
Comanche
Sioux
Up to 2 ft odorata 'Eugene de
Land'

Arc-en-Ciel
Phoebus
Up to 2½ ft Livingstone

MARGINAL PLANTS

Subjects suitable for planting in small garden pools of up to about 24 sq. ft surface area. The heights given are those of a mature plant. The depths at which all succeed vary, but are within the 0"-9" of water scale, obviously smaller growing plants preferring the shallower water, whilst the taller are equally at home in both.

Acorus gramineus	9 ins	*Menyanthes tri-*	
A. *pusillus*	9 ins	*foliata*	9 ins-1 ft
A. *pusillus*		*Mimulus ringens*	1-1½ ft
'Variegatus'	9 ins	M. 'Whitecroft	
Alisma parviflora	1½-2 ft	Scarlet'	2-4 ins
A. *natans*	floating foliage	*Myosotis scor-*	
A. *ranunculoides*	6 ins	*pioides* and	
Calla palustris	9 ins	cultivars	6-9 ins
Caltha palustris		*Narthecium ossi-*	
and varieties	1-1½ ft	*fragum*	6-9 ins
C. *leptosepala*	1-1½ ft	*Peltandra virginica*	1½-2 ft
Cotula		P. *alba*	1½-2 ft
coronopifolia	6-9 ins	*Phragmites com-*	
Cyperus vegetus	2-2½ ft	*munis var.*	
Damasonium		*variegatus*	1½-2 ft
alisma	9 ins	*Preslia cervina*	6-9 ins
Eriophorum		*Ranunculus flam-*	
augustifolium	1-1½ ft	*mula* and forms	6-9 ins
Houttynia cordata		*Saggittaria*	
and 'Plena'	9 ins	*sagittifolia* and	
Hypericum elodes	6-9 ins	*japonica*	9 ins-1½ ft
Iris laevigata		*Saururus cernuus*	1 ft
varieties and		*Triglochin*	
cultivars	1½-3 ft	*palustris*	9 ins-1 ft
I. *versicolor* and		*Typha laxmannii*	3-4 ft
cultivars	1½-3 ft	T. *minima*	1-1½ ft
Juncus effusus		*Veronica*	
'Spiralis'	1 ft	*beccabunga*	6-9 ins
J.e. 'Vittatus'	1 ft		

Subjects suitable for the average garden pool and smaller natural pond.

Acorus calamus	3-5 ft	A. *parviflora*	1½-2 ft
A.c. 'Variegatus'	3 ft	A. *natans*	floating foliage
Alisma plantago-		*Anemonopsis*	
aquatica	3 ft	*californica*	2 ft

Butomus umbel-		*Mentha aquatica*	1-1½ ft
latus	2-3 ft	*Menyanthes tri-*	
Calla palustris	9 ins	*foliata*	9 ins-1 ft
Caltha palustris		*Mimulus ringens*	1-1½ ft
and varieties	1-1½ ft	*M. luteus* and	
C. leptosepala	1-1½ ft	cultivars	9 ins-1 ft
C. polypetala	3 ft	*Myosotis*	
Carex pendula		*scorpiodes* and	
C. riparia 'Bowles		cultivars	6-9 ins
Golden'	2½ ft	*Nasturtium*	
C.r. 'Variegata'	2½ ft	*officinale*	6 ins-1 ft
Cotula coronopi-		*Peltandra virginica*	1½-2 ft
folia	6-9 ins	*P. alba*	1½-2 ft
Cyperus vegetus	2-2½ ft	*Phragmites com-*	
C. longus	2-4 ft	*munis var.*	
Damasonium		*variegatus*	1½-2 ft
alisma	9 ins	*Polgonum*	
Eriophorum		*amphibium*	floating foliage
angustifolium	1-1½ ft	*Pontederia cordata*	2-3 ft
E. latifolium	1-2 ft	*Preslia cervina*	6-9 ins
Glyceria aquatica		*Ranunculus flammula* and	
variegata	2-3 ft	forms	6-9 ins
Houttynia cordata	6-9 ins	*R. lingua*	2-4 ft
H.c. 'Plena'	6-9 ins	*R.l.* 'Grandiflora'	2-4 ft
Hypericum elodes	6-9 ins	*Sagittaria*	
Iris laevigata and		*sagittifolia* and	
varieties and		*japonica*	9 ins-1½ ft
cultivars	1½-3 ft	*Saururus cernuus*	1 ft
I. pseudacorus		*Scirpus lacustris*	2-4 ft
and forms and		*S. tabernaemon-*	
cultivars	2-4 ft	*tani* and forms	2-4 ft
I. versicolor and		*Typha laxmannii*	3-4 ft
cultivars	1½-3 ft	*T. minima*	1-1½ ft
Juncus effusus		*Veronica*	
'Spiralis'	1 ft	*beccabunga*	6-9 ins
J.e. 'Vittatus'	1 ft		

Subjects suitable for planting in large natural pools or lakes.

Acorus calamus	3-5 ft	*C. leptosepala*	1-1½ ft
Alisma plantago		*C. polypetala*	3 ft
aquatica	3 ft	*Carex pseudo-*	
Butomus umbel-		*cyperus*	3-3½ ft
latus	2-3 ft	*C. riparia*	3 ft
Caltha palustris		*C.r.* 'Bowles	
and varieties	1-1½ ft	Golden'	2½ ft

C.r. 'Variegata'	2½ ft	*Phragmites com-*	
C. pendula	3 ft	*munis*	3-6 ft
Decodon verticil-		*P.c. var.*	
latus	3-4 ft	*variegatus*	1½-2 ft
Eriophorum		*Polygonum*	
angustifolium	1-1½ ft	*amphibium*	floating foliage
E. latifolium	1-2 ft	*Pontederia cordata*	2-3 ft
Glyceria aquatica		*Preslia cervina*	6-9 ins
variegata	2-3 ft	*Ranunculus lingua*	2-4 ft
Hippuris vulgaris	1-1½ ft	*R.I. 'Grandiflora'*	2-4 ft
Iris laevigata and		*Rumex hydrola-*	
varieties and		*pathum*	6-8 ft
cultivars	1½-3 ft	*Sagittaria*	
I. pseudacorus		*sagittifolia* and	
and forms and		*japonica*	9 ins-1½ ft
cultivars	2-4 ft	*S. latifolia* and	
I. versicolor and		forms	4-5 ft
cultivars	1½-3 ft	*Scirpus lacustris*	2-4 ft
Ludwigia palustris	1 ft	*S. tabernaemon-*	
Mentha aquatica	1-1½ ft	*tani* and forms	2-4 ft
Menyanthes tri-		*Sparganium*	
foliata	9 ins-1 ft	*ramosum*	2-4 ft
Mimulus ringens	1-1½ ft	*Typha angustifolia*	6-8 ft
M. luteus	1-1½ ft	*T. latifolia*	6-8 ft
Myosotis		*T. truxillensis*	8-10 ft
scorpiodes and		*T. laxmannii*	3-4 ft
cultivars	6-9 ins	*Veronica*	
Nasturtium		*beccabunga*	6-9 ins
officinale	6 ins-1 ft	*Zizania aquatica*	8-10 ft
Peltandra virginica	1½-2 ft	*Z. latifolia*	4-5 ft
P. alba	1½-2 ft		

FLOATING PLANTS

The type of pool to which the following submerged subjects are suited best is indicated as follows:—

S=Small   M=Medium   L=Large

Azolla ssp	S M L	*Trapa natans*	S M
Hydrocharis ssp	S M L	*Utricularia* ssp	S M
Lemna trisulca	S M	*Wolffia arrhiza*	S
Stratiotes aloides	S M L		

SUBMERGED OXYGENATING PLANTS

The type of pool to which the following submerged subjects are suited best is indicated as follows:—

S=Small   M=Medium   L=Large

Apium inundatum	S	M	L	*Isoetes lacustris*	S	M	L
A. nodiflorum			L	*Lagarosiphon major*	S	M	L
Callitriche ssp	S	M	L	*Lobelia dortmanna*	S	M	L
Ceratophyllum ssp	S	M	L	*Myriophyllum* ssp	S	M	L
Chara aspera	S	M	L	*Oeonanthe fluviatilis*			L
Eleocharis acicularis	S	M		*Potomogeton crispus*	S	M	L
Elodea ssp		M	L	*Potomogeton* all			
Fontinalis				other ssp		M	L
antipyretica		M	L	*Ranunculus aquatilis*	S	M	L
Hottonia inflata		M	L	*Tillaea recurva*	S	M	L
H. palustris		M	L				

Appendix

METRIC CONVERSION

With the advent of metrication it is advisable to be aware of a few metric equivalents appertaining to depth and height.

inches	centimetres	feet	metres
1	2.54	1	0.305
2	5.08	2	0.610
3	7.62	3	0.914
4	10.16	4	1.219
5	12.70	5	1.524
6	15.24	6	1.829
7	17.78	7	2.134
8	20.32	8	2.438
9	22.86	9	2.743
10	25.40	10	3.048
11	27.94		
12	30.48		
18	45.72		

CALCULATING CAPACITIES

RECTANGULAR POOLS (OR AQUARIA): Multiply length by width by depth (all in feet) to obtain volume in cubic feet. Multiply this by 6.25 to give the capacity in gallons.

CIRCULAR POOLS: Multiply depth in feet by the square of the diameter in feet by 4.9 to give approximate gallonage.

EASY REFERENCE TABLE FOR RECTANGULAR POOLS

Capacity of rectangular pools *one foot* average depth.

GALLONS (Imperial)

BREADTH (ft.)	2	4	6	LENGTH (ft.) 8	10	12	16
2	25	50	75	100	125	150	200
3	38	75	112	150	186	275	300
4	50	100	150	200	250	300	400
5	62	125	186	250	310	375	500
6	75	150	225	300	375	450	600

EASY REFERENCE TABLE FOR CIRCULAR POOLS

Capacity of circular garden pools. GALLONS (Imperial)

DIAMETER IN FEET	12	AVERAGE DEPTH OF WATER IN INCHES 18	24	30	36
4	78	117	156	195	234
6	176	264	352	440	528
8	313	470	626	783	939
10	489	734	978	1223	1467
12	705	1058	1410	1763	2115

EASY REFERENCE TABLE FOR AQUARIUMS

SIZE OF AQUARIUM (INCHES)			APPROXIMATE CAPACITY		
			Imperial	U.S.	
Length	Width	Height	gallons	gallons	litres
16	8	8	3	4	18
18	10	10	5	6	27
24	12	12	10	12	54
24	12	15	13	15	67
36	12	15	20	23	103
48	15	15	36	40	180
72	15	18	65	75	315

VOLUME—RATE OF FLOW
An important factor when installing a fountain or waterfall.

Gallons per minute	Gallons per hour	Litres per minute	Litres per hour
1	60	4.55	272.7
2	120	9.09	545.5
3	180	13.64	818.3
4	240	18.18	1091
5	300	22.73	1363
6	360	27.27	1636
7	420	31.82	1909
8	480	36.37	2182
9	540	40.91	2454
10	600	45.46	2727
11	660	50.00	3000
12	720	54.55	3273
13	780	59.10	3545
14	840	63.64	3818
15	900	68.10	4091
16	960	72.74	4364
17	1020	77.28	4636
18	1080	81.83	4909
19	1140	86.38	5182
20	1200	90.92	5455

TEMPERATURE CONVERSION
To convert centigrade (°C) to Fahrenheit (°F) multiply by 9, divide by 5 and add 32.

To convert Fahrenheit (°F) to centigrade (°C) deduct 32, multiply by 5, and divide by 9.

Some useful equivalents

°F	°C	°F	°C
32	0	60	15.5
40	4.4	65	18.3
50	10	70	21.1
75	23.8	90	32.2
80	26.6	100	37.8
85	29.4	212	100

OTHER USEFUL INFORMATION
One Imperial gallon of water occupies 0.16 cubic feet and weighs 10 lb.

One U.S. gallon is equivalent to 0.83268 Imperial gallon and weighs 8.3 lb.

One cubic foot of water is equivalent to 6.24 gallons or 28.3 litres and weighs 62.32 lbs.

One Imperial gallon of water contains approximately 90,000 drops.

One Imperial gallon equals 160 fluid ounces or 4.546 litres.

One litre equals 1.76 pints or 0.22 Imperial gallons or 35.196 fluid ounces.

4 teaspoonfuls are the equivalent to 2 dessertspoonfuls, 1 tablespoonful or ½ ounce.

Index